MY HALF ORANGE

A Story of Love and Language in Seville

MY HALF ORANGE

A Story of Love and Language in Seville

by John Julius Reel

Tortoise Books

Chicago

FIRST EDITION, APRIL 2023

©2023 John Julius Reel

Published in the United States by Tortoise Books.
www.tortoisebooks.com

ISBN: 978-1-948954-77-8

This book is a memoir and is drawn from the author's experience and recollections going back many years. Dialogue is approximate and appears in quotation marks for the benefit of the reader. For readability, in some cases events and sequences have been compressed. On occasion, names and identifying details have been changed to protect privacy.

Illustrations by Daniel Rosell
Cover image by Isidoro Borrego Moreno
Tortoise Books Logo ©2023 by Tortoise Books.
Logo artwork by Rachele O'Hare.

Vine buscando cobre y encontré oro.
(I came looking for copper and found gold.)

—Spanish saying

PROLOGUE

NUESTRA HUMILDE MORADA
(Our Humble Abode)

It's quiet at the moment, so I can concentrate. The boys are old enough now to be in school. In a couple of hours, my wife and I will start preparing their lunch so that it's hot on the table when they get home. Meanwhile, she's taking advantage of the morning by doing yoga in our bedroom. I can hear the mantras through the door. I know she's got the bed pushed aside, and looming over her is an elaborate, life-like depiction of Christ on the cross, way too big considering the dimensions of the room and the lapsed Catholicism of the couple who sleep beneath it, but it's hung there since her parents bought and furnished the place forty-five years ago here on the outskirts of Seville, Spain. Before that they lived in a small town in the Sierra Norte (the northern foothills), about twenty-five miles away, where my future wife attended a convent school, learning to meditate by praying the rosary with the nuns every morning. The mantra has changed but not her habits. Christ has always figured in my life, too, a shining example of selflessness and guts. So the garish cross isn't going anywhere.

Our older boy's room is just to the right. For a few years after my wife's parents passed on, this room became my study; then the boys reached the age to want separate rooms, so I gave it up. The one heirloom that my son decided to keep was a framed black and white photograph of his paternal grandfather as a young man, wearing a suit and sitting in what looks to be an empty airport lounge, with an ankle propped on his knee, creating a platform for the tabloid newspaper spread open before him. A cup of coffee sits within reach on the floor, and he holds a lit cigarette while looking over his shoulder at a handsome, gray-haired man draped in a beige overcoat who's come over to talk to him.

The man is James L. Buckley, a former US senator. I know this because Buckley has signed the photo. I know that the tabloid on my dad's lap is the New York *Daily News*, because that's the paper he wrote for. I know the year is 1970, because that's the year Buckley ran his successful senatorial campaign, which my dad, as a reporter, covered. The back page headline reads, CAN ALI MAKE IT BACK? That October, Muhammad Ali had been readmitted to boxing after a three-and-a-half-year ban for draft evasion during the Vietnam War. He would make it back all right. My dad was thirty-one, on his way to becoming a well-known New York columnist. I was three. By far the most touching detail in the photo are the Band-Aids on the tips of each of my dad's fingers. My mom was on his back about biting his fingernails. The Band-Aids were his way to break the habit, and it did the trick.

In the hallway, a six-tiered, blood-red bookcase goes straight up to the ceiling. Here I reserve a shelf for the few books that I brought with me from the States, books that once fueled my spiritual wanderlust: Mailer, Miller (Henry), Thompson (Hunter S.), Kerouac, Bowles, McCarthy (Mary), and Duras. I hope to reread them one day, with the wisdom of the years. Also prominently placed, with its battered spine reinforced by duct tape, is *The Reading Lesson: Teach Your Child to Read in 20 Easy Lessons*, by Michael Levin, M.D., and Charan Langton, M.S., gifted pedagogues both. I used their method to teach my boys to read in English before they went to school. Contrary to what I used to think before moving here, languages are not learned through osmosis. They've got to be—in the gentlest sense of the expression—forced down our throats. So, for fifteen minutes a day, starting from age four, the boys sat down with me, sounding out the letters and words on the page until we could move on to story books. Even now, after a half-dozen years in Spanish public schools, they still prefer to address and speak to each other in English. Although *The Reading Lesson* has long since served its purpose, I keep it here, a reminder that I'm a teacher, even at home.

In the salon is a big table whose thick skirts brush the floor, with a heater beneath. This, the *mesa camilla*, a staple in Andalusian

With best regards
James Bru

homes for centuries, is where the woman of our house takes a load off between the months of October and March. Homes and apartment blocks in this part of the world are built to keep heat at bay, not to maintain it, so even mild winters can get chilly indoors, unless you're sitting around the *mesa camilla*. The rest of us come and go, snuggling up next to the *materfamilias*, then returning toasty warm and reassured to our projects and pastimes. Orbiting around her calm, cozy, always accessible presence, we are at peace. We are one. If we ever forget that, we're lost, every single one of us.

On the opposite side of the salon sits a beige orthopedic armchair. First my father-in-law, for whom we bought it, and then my mother-in-law spent way too much of their final few years confined to it. Every evening for two of those years, I lifted my father-in-law out of the chair into a wheelchair, brought him into the bathroom, and then to bed. Our daily interaction, for as long as it lasted, anchored me more than having children, who were then too young to really need me. Near the end, he developed an ornery and insistent open wound on his heel. Every morning, my sister-in-law would clean and wrap it, and I would do the same in the evening, but the wrapping always came undone in between. To this day, faint blood stains remain on the armchair's footrest, reminding me of his pain, of family pains, and of our efforts to alleviate them—efforts I hadn't known I was capable of.

Finally there's the terrace, where during the evenings my father-in-law, when alive and well, would go to smoke his Fortunas, listen to sports radio on his hand-held transistor, and end up annoying neighbors all up and down the courtyard with his snores. Following his example, I retreat here to get away from family noise, content to look out over our tiny corner of Seville. Simply put, love brought and keeps me here. Past the courtyard gate is the bus stop where our boys catch the 11 to go to school and I catch the 13 to go to work. Across the street is La Bodeguita Chari, where we can buy milk, bread, and cold cuts in a pinch. To the left is an auto repair shop. The owner, Luis, is a decent and honest mechanic as long as you don't need your car for a couple of weeks. Just out of sight, on the corner, is a busy café bar with a dozen zinc-topped tables out front. Once, when my wife was thirteen years old, she stood on that bustling corner shouting, "¡*Viejo verde! ¡Asqueroso!*" (Dirty old man! Disgusting!) over and over at the top of her lungs at a neighbor who had put his hands all over her older sister in the building elevator the day before.

My wife was made to meditate, embody warmth, and be the calm center of a loving home, but she will transform into a virago in order to defend her own, among whom I am now blessed to count myself.

She's the cornerstone. Hard to believe that for thirty-eight years I didn't know of her existence.

BEFORE THE REVOLUTION

UNSENT

At the age of thirty-seven, I was living in ancient Barrio Santa Cruz in a rented room, pining for my much younger American ex-girlfriend who had dumped me only a few weeks before. That had not been among the considered outcomes when I had dropped everything except her to set out for my sojourn in Seville three months earlier.

Things could not have gone better when she'd come over for a visit. We had wept in each other's arms upon saying goodbye at the ticketed-passengers-only boundary point of San Pablo Airport. Now it occurred to me that her tears were because she had known it was over but did not want to tell me, just like I did not want to tell her when I would be returning from my sojourn. I was leaving that wide open.

Friends told me that she was going out with someone else within two weeks of her return to New York. Talk about a wake-up call... sort of like the one I was receiving right now: José, the bilingual expat who ran the rooming house I lived in, was scraping the burnt part of his toast off with a knife. Every single morning, that was what I woke to. *Chsss! Chsss! Chsss!* When would José learn to toast his bread a little less?

Every night was just as bad, reality just as mind-numbingly hard to believe. I would go to bed only after checking my email one more time—this was January 2006, before smartphones made all communication instant—to see if she had finally answered me. Before that, I would have addressed yet another blank postcard to her, placed a stamp on it, and walked down to the main branch of the Sevillian post office to put it in the slot marked *EXTRANJERO* (foreign), the thick brass rim of the opening looking like a puppet's mouth laughing at me.

That was my plan to get her back, or at least to keep her from forgetting me. One postcard every single day for eternity, if necessary. Even if she threw it in the garbage, she would have to touch it first. There I would be, held by her, if only for a moment, insisting, letting her know that I was not going anywhere. Of course, I had already gone somewhere, to Spain. Perhaps I should be letting her know when she could expect me home. But what if she no longer wanted me no matter where I was?

On the walk back to the rooming house, through the narrow, winding, cobblestoned streets of one of the largest and best-preserved old towns in Europe, sometimes I would shed tears of self-pity, or of heartbreak, or of rage (mostly rage) at myself, for becoming reduced to this state. Had I not come to Spain to live, in the most expansive sense? Ten years of teaching college composition, ten years of writing but not getting published (perhaps because I had nothing interesting to say), ten years of—let's be honest—girlfriends who never got older, while I got ever closer to forty. Maybe, against my will, by becoming my ex, she had finally liberated me. But how could that be if I couldn't let her go? She was everywhere I looked.

José, in his early fifties and born and raised in Puerto Rico, oversaw the rooming house with his wife, Lena, almost twenty years older and from Tennessee. He was a former computer technician, recently trained as a hypnotherapist; she was a former PhD candidate in psychology, now interested in Jungian astrology. She was a writer as well, which was how we'd hit it off. A few days into my now ex-girlfriend's month-long visit, we had interviewed with José and Lena, looking to rent a room. Age difference in romantic relationships was clearly something that we had in common. Perhaps that's why we had made the cut.

José and Lena agreed to rent us their room, the master bedroom, while they visited the States for a month during the Christmas holidays. José would later say that we had "held down the fort"—an apt phrase, because we really had holed up there, getting lost more in each other than in Seville. When they returned, we repaired to one of the smaller rooms to cling even more tightly to each other before the imminent farewell. It got to the point where I just wanted to get the goodbyes over with and get on with my adventure, although we made vague plans for her to visit again in the summer.

Once she left, Lena and I became confidants. Lena told me about her childhood, enriched by her Cherokee roots, and about her first husband who, aside from a daughter, had given her nothing but grief. Now she worried that her daughter had perpetuated the family curse of the women marrying and having children with men who were impossible to respect. As for my situation, she told me about an affair she once had with her professor, how it was one of the happiest, headiest times of her life, while it lasted.

She added, "The sooner we get these things out of our system, the better."

One weekend morning, I woke at 6 a.m., unable to sleep. I opened my laptop and logged into my email to see if my ex had written to me, but of course nothing, just like six hours earlier. All of a sudden, the postcard game seemed futile. I needed some form of encouragement, no matter how meager. In a frantic attempt to get it, I poured out my heart in an email, the first I had written in what seemed like months, although it could not have been more than two weeks. I explained the pains I had taken not to write to her, that I saw the city as only a backdrop to our love, constantly reminding me of us. I wrote that I was stunned and heartbroken by her silence, but also angry and determined—determined, I said, to wait for her. She would always be in love with me, whether she knew it or not.

"Mark my words," I wrote.

Before I could retract anything, I clicked send, then got up, heart racing, to go make some breakfast. As I passed the dining room, there was Lena, sitting at the table, the very picture of a living oracle: wild gray hair and a long, owlish face, like something chiseled into wood. I sat across from her and told her what I had just sent off, reciting the email almost word for word. She listened patiently, until I was done. In the silence that followed, she bent her head as if to swallow something lodged in her throat, then raised her eyes again.

"Can you unsend it?" she said.

If only I had struck up this conversation as a prelude to asking Lena for a stamp. If only I had written a letter and still held it in my hand.

"José knows about computers," she added. "Maybe he can help you."

José had been listening from the kitchen.

"You can only unsend it if you both have the same internet provider and she hasn't opened it yet," he called out.

My ex and I both had AOL. It was 1:30 a.m. in the States. I doubted that she was up reading emails.

"Do the right thing," said Lena. "*Déjala en paz.*" (Leave her in peace.)

In the kitchen, José started scraping off the charred part of the toast. *Chsss! Chsss! Chsss!*

I went back to my room and unsent the email. I shut the postcards up in a drawer. Leave her in peace… leave her alone… in peace… alone. Those two ideas were synonymous in English, but not in Spanish. In Spanish, *dejar solo* (to leave alone) had nothing to do with *dejar en paz* (to leave in peace). She had been left in peace, and I had been left alone.

RECEIVING MY SOUL

My room had a single small window, looking out on a tiny inner patio, completely bare, maybe twelve by fifteen feet, which belonged to the apartment on the ground floor. The patio was always shut tight, as though hermetically sealed, except for the circular drain at its center. Out of that drain at night emerged the most savvy and evasive strain of mosquitos that I had ever had the displeasure of being harassed by. They would somehow enter my room, perhaps through the air vent, or through the crack under my door. I never did figure it out. All I knew was that, ten minutes after lights out, I would begin to hear one or two of them buzzing around my head. After slapping unsuccessfully at my ear, I would sit up, exasperated, and flip on the light. Two or three of them would be poised on my white stucco walls, taunting me. Upon sensing the approach of my hand, they would dive-bomb to the mottled greyish-beige marble floor, which served as their camouflage, laying low until I gave up and turned out the lights again. Then they would rise up and resume the hunt. Not until morning, when they would be fat, drunk, and careless after having gotten their fill of me, did I ever manage to make any kills. The stains were proof. When I finally moved out, I left behind the blank postcards and walls speckled with my blood— my contribution to Barrio Santa Cruz, a neighborhood that, on the surface at least, had remained largely unchanged for over six hundred years.

The thing about expat life is that you can't really make friends, or, if you do, they will soon be gone, like Lena and José. One day, Lena felt a general ache in her bones that did not go away. It got more acute. She lost her energy to join José on excursions. Finally, they returned to the States to see a specialist. Turned out she was shot through with cancer. In one of her last emails to me, when she knew she had only months to live and wanted to offer me the job of running the rooming house, she asked if I recalled the astrological chart she had done for herself, and the life-changing event that was supposed to happen to her that year, and how excited she had been to find out what it was.

"Well, I found out," she wrote. "I predicted my own death without realizing it."

In the end, I declined to run the rooming house. The last thing I wanted was to recruit and watch over a constantly rotating list of long-stay tourists, even if that meant free lodging and a stipend that covered almost all other expenses.

I had already started working, teaching conversational English to Sevillian adults, to whom I would complain about how incompetently I spoke their native tongue. One day, a student at the engineering company where I taught on weekday mornings suggested that I do a language exchange with her coworker, who wanted to improve her English. The idea would be to meet up once or twice a week, speaking half the time in her native language and half the time in mine. I was intrigued. I had seen my student's coworker using the office copy machine next to the conference room where I gave classes. Seeing her there and noticing how beautiful she was made me think it might be time to start dating again.

Immediately after class, I headed for her department and walked boldly up to her desk.

"I hear you're looking for a speaking partner in English," I said.

She calmly looked up from her work. Seeing her big Berber eyes and straight dark hair, parted in the middle, I thought of *Pocahontas* (the Disney version), with me in the role of hunky Captain John Smith. She didn't have to know what I was thinking to put me right in my place.

"Yes, someone with a British accent," she said. "Do you know anyone?"

I could hear guffaws being suppressed in nearby cubicles.

"But I have an American accent," I said, as though guilty of something.

"*Estadounidense,*" she said, correcting me.

Fair enough. In Spain, America did not only mean the United States.

I pressed on.

"Want to meet this weekend?"

She shook her head. "Maybe next weekend."

She returned to her work, and I walked away praying that in the next ten days she didn't find some posh, lock-jawed Limey to practice English and drink gin and tonics with.

Turned out she preferred beer. We finally met at Gambrinus, a Spanish beer bar chain, in the mall down the road from her office building. The pints of Cruzcampo (Sevillians' beer of choice), as well as a desire to impress her, loosened my tongue. Not for months afterward would I again reach such Spanish-speaking heights, a good thing, perhaps even my salvation, because it kept me from slipping in the type of snide remarks that might have put her off. I should say that my memory of that first meeting is clouded by what I had yet to understand about communicating in any language, no matter how well or poorly spoken: almost everything depends on the listener. I have since seen people with only rudimentary Spanish—my brother, for instance—sit down for a conversation with my now wife and walk away believing they are fluent. No doubt on that first date the revelation that I could actually hold my own in Spanish had more to do with the fact that someone could finally understand me, or chose to allow me to think she did.

That may explain how, in only a few short months, we were a couple, and she would sit with me for sometimes three-hour stretches in local cafés as I scribbled things down in a notebook. We would hardly speak. She would be reading and thinking, sometimes underlining passages in her book, sometimes staring off into space. She never seemed anxious or ill at ease. I would be the one who got sudden urges to leave, wanting to be behind closed doors with her.

One day, on the way back to her place, we stopped at the local greengrocer's. The woman in front of us put down her overflowing shopping bags to pay, and I, wanting to prove helpful, piped up, "*Señora, se han caído tus peras.*" (Ma'am, your pears have fallen.)

Turned out that by saying "your pears" instead of "the pears," I was referring to her breasts. My new guide and guardian, ever at the ready, added, "*Las mías también. Los años no perdonan,*" (Mine too. The years take their toll,) and that way everybody could have a good laugh, but not entirely at the expense of the *guiri*—what the Spanish call a fair-skinned foreigner.

This incident and others like it confirmed what was more difficult to deny every day, that this was the woman for me, a companion both when I got lost in my imagination and when reality pinned me down.

She had helped me settle into a new rented room, taking me to "*el chino*" (the Chinaman's) and "*el moro*" (the Moor's) in her neighborhood to get cheap carpets and wall tapestries to give my new twelve cubic meters of personal space across town a touch of personal warmth. It was my fourth move in fourteen months, this time to a shared apartment with an old New York friend and a Parisian obsessed with the NBA, although I ended up spending very little time with them.

A French woman who worked for the same company as my new constant companion had tried to put me off her by saying, "She's older than she looks," but that only made me want her more. Not since freshman year in college had I dated someone my own age. As cool as ever, this full-fledged *sevillana* didn't seem to need anything from me, not even my presence, yet was always available when I called. Only our language exchange was falling apart, or rather the English-speaking side of it. Once, when I corrected her, explaining that "terrific" had nothing to do with "terror" and was actually synonymous with "fantastic" or "wonderful," she made me prove it to her with a dictionary. Clearly she was not and would never be my student. I guessed that was a move in the right direction.

When I finally told her that I wanted to break up with her as an English teacher so we could carry on happily as a couple, I added, "Best not to shit where we sleep."

She waggled a defiant finger at me.

"*Lo que se dice en español es más bonito: En casa del herrero, cuchara de palo.*" (What we say in Spanish is more beautiful: In the blacksmith's house, wooden spoons.)

"The cobbler's children go barefoot" popped into my head, but that saying seemed to imply that the cobbler should practice what he preaches. The Spanish version was more sympathetic, implying that a guy deserved a break. Spanish, then, by all means. Besides, better if she showed *me* the way. I had come to Spain to learn.

The first time she brought me to the defunct coal town that she was raised in, Villanueva del Río y Minas (New Town of the River and Mines), I marveled at the antique machinery and crumbling chimneys that towered up from the valleys in the undulating landscape. One rusted, hulking structure was crowned with a stork's nest, with two of the big-beaked birds preening atop the skeletal remains. An abandoned, dilapidated mansion, perhaps the former home of a coal baron, situated on the corner of the plaza where we ate stale bar sandwiches, was now occupied by a band of gypsy squatters. A group of small children stood at the edge of the plaza, staring at us. Had the woman across from me once resembled these wide-eyed waifs? She seemed to take all this for granted.

A hundred yards away stood the town hall, once the Marist Brothers Catholic school that her father had attended until eighth grade when he dropped out to work, doing odd jobs with his five older brothers so the family could make ends meet. The Anthem of Andalusia rang out on perpetual repeat from megaphone speakers attached to the flagpole out front. It was February 28, 2007, Andalusia Day. Tellingly enough, one year and two days later, our firstborn would come into the world, and we would name him after Blas Infante, who wrote the lyrics to that anthem: "*Los andaluces queremos/.../ hombres de luz, que a los hombres,/ alma de hombres les dimos.*" (Andalusians want men of light... and to give these men of light their souls.)

By late May, when she and I were living together, we returned to her hometown so I could meet her parents, Luis and María. They had an apartment in Seville but spent most weekends in "*Las Minas,*" in the house that Luis's brothers had built for their mother seventy years earlier, when Luis had been only nine and their father had recently succumbed to black lung. Luis would inherit the place in the end because his brothers had wanted him to.

I walked through the front door. The walls were bastions of stone, mortar, and plaster at least two feet thick, marked by dark stains of humidity from groundwater seeping up from the terracotta floor.

I'm in love with a cavewoman, I thought.

Luis, enfeebled by heart disease by then, perhaps already in the incipient stages of Parkinson's (in the final stages, he would end up teaching me so much), sat in the cool, damp center room, watching the bullfights on a cathode-ray tube TV with poor reception. I sat down next to him, and he waved a hand dismissively at the picture.

"*Son muy malos,*" (They're very bad,) he said about the bullfighters, kindly assuming I knew enough to understand what that meant.

María, squat and blockish with a helmet of bottle-brown hair (soon one of her crusades would be to foist Grecian Formula on me), offset her husband's stillness. My *sevillana* had warned me about her. "*Es un manojo de nervios.*" (She's a bundle of nerves.) To welcome me, she brought in a half-frozen liter bottle of orange Fanta and a glass, banged them down in front of me, and motioned that I should help myself. I stood and bowed as though in Japan. Speaking comprehensible Spanish to anyone besides their daughter was still beyond me. Hand signals and strained facial expressions would have to do.

I screwed off the top of the bottle. *PHTTT!* Its contents bubbled up and spilled over, fizzing onto the table and floor. María popped up from the sofa and lunged to snatch the bottle out of my dripping hands, frantically shaking her head to downplay the accident. In case I didn't understand, as she backed into the kitchen, she overturned the bottle to intentionally dump more soda on the floor. Seconds later, she burst triumphantly back on the scene with a mop and bucket, inviting me to observe, as if maybe I had never seen such a household instrument before, or certainly not so deftly employed.

Luis looked at me with a conspiratorial smirk, as if to say, "Welcome to my world."

Later, María would pull me aside and say, "*Mi hija no es una guarra*," which meant either "My daughter isn't a dirt bag" or "My daughter isn't depraved."

I nodded emphatically. Either way, I couldn't have approved more.

Not a bad reception, I thought, from two people supposedly set against me.

In the States, I had never lived with a woman, afraid that it would interfere with my routine. I hadn't considered that I might create a new routine, a shared routine that would make my life more significant. My *sevillana* had cleaned out three drawers for my stuff. She would have cleaned out more, but that was all I needed. I put my things away, then shut the drawers, and nothing seemed to have changed, but of course it had, especially for her, who had been living here alone, happily enough, before I had appeared at her work cubicle one morning with a shaky proposition. I recalled how, back in New York, after cleaning my apartment, I used to joke with friends that now all I had to do was get rid of myself, and the place would be ideal for habitation. I hoped she would never think that.

I tried to think what was waiting for me back home. Hang-ups and uncertainty, mostly. I would miss my parents, of course, but not how I responded to their influence. For so many years, all my life really, I had lived under the shadow of my father's success. He had been a newspaper man in New York City for thirty-eight years and a columnist for twenty-six. When I was ten years old, the image of him pounding away on his Underwood had appeared on the sides of all New York *Daily News* trucks, under the words, "William Reel Wednesday & Friday." In his heyday, New Yorkers had read my dad as eagerly as they had tabloid legends like Pete Hamill and Jimmy Breslin. To other people, I had always been "Bill Reel's son."

That had weighed on me, and not just as a writer. For example, moving in with a woman before marriage contradicted his rules of acceptable moral behavior. Even as I approached forty, these rules still held sway over me. But living abroad freed me up enough to take this step. My parents would find out I was living with a woman only after I told them that we were expecting, at which point, according to them, *not* living with her would have been unacceptable moral behavior. Somehow I had, as the Spanish say, *arrimado el ascua a mi sardina* (brought the coal ember closer to my sardine), which meant working the system to my advantage.

Even so, to leave a certain version of myself behind forever, I would need a final nudge. One day, alone in Sevillian residence number four before settling in with my *media naranja* (half orange) to be fruitful and multiply, I opened my email and saw that my ex had written to me. More than a year had passed. She said she would like to try again. She missed me and had saved all my postcards. At the very least she wanted to keep in touch, because who knew what the future held.

In the past, I had preferred to string along my exes, always hedging my bets. This time I played things straight. I wrote that I missed her, too, that I would always cherish our times together, but that I had found someone I needed to give my complete and undivided attention to. I wrote my response instantly, absolutely sure of my instincts, not caring that I had nobody to discuss the consequences with, although I did recall Lena in that moment, and tried to evoke her spirit, asking her to help align my stars.

Then I pressed send.

TWO PICNICS

My *media naranja* (half orange), which is how the Spanish say "soulmate," was sitting across from me on the terrace of El Guardita (The Little Gamekeeper), a tavern at the top of the hill at the southwestern entrance to *Las Minas*. It was a place that drew hunting parties after the hunt. If you enter an Andalusian watering hole and see a bunch of tables pushed together with fifteen to twenty guys sitting around the makeshift groaning board, wearing camouflage clothes and dusty boots and feasting on platters piled with meat, take that as a sign that the food is good—nothing fancy, but skillfully and wholesomely prepared. We had ordered our favorite dish, Plato Lucio, named after a famous restaurant in Madrid. It was just fried potatoes and eggs, all mixed together, and sprinkled with chorizo. After this, I would be too full to eat anything else for the rest of the day. It was three o'clock, Spanish lunch time. We had ordered mugs of beer. Our two small boys were standing at the terrace railing, with some hunks of stale bread that the waitress had given them to feed the chickens below, the same chickens who had laid the eggs to provide us with a good portion of our meal.

"Is *media naranja* a corny term?" I asked my now wife.

She leaned back in her chair, lifting her face to the warm winter sun.

"No," she said. "It's common enough."

"Except for one random Spanish teacher," I said, "I don't think I've ever heard it in the mouth of a native. 'Soulmate' can be kind of corny. You don't hear it much."

"Maybe because hardly anybody finds theirs." She gave a nod toward the kitchen, run by the wife, and then toward the bar, kept by the husband, together since middle school. My wife had roamed the town streets with them thirty-five years ago. "So many people seem sick and tired of the people they've chosen to spend their lives with."

"But not us, right?" I said.

"That depends on how many of these we drink," she said, raising her frosty mug. "*Salud*, soulmate." She took a big swallow.

"Seriously," I said. "At what point exactly did you know that you could spend the rest of your life with me?"

"I don't work that way, *cariño* (dear)," she said. "I had faith in us from the start, and haven't been disappointed yet."

"Yet, huh?"

"I'm just saying I live in the moment."

"Right, and I live in my head—which has changed, by the way."

"Gotten bigger and thicker?"

"Spanish has altered my way of thinking," I said, "how I see the world…how I see you, even. Words mean something different now. Take the word 'orange.' Remember the first two picnics we went on together?"

"That one in the Alamillo, right? I can't believe I allowed you to take me there. I must have been *embobada* (silly in love)."

Parque del Alamillo, Seville's biggest park, had a patch of orange trees at the edge of it, planted in neat rows, a remnant of the orchards that had once rimmed the old city. I had thought it would be romantic if she and I laid a blanket down in the middle of it, with wine and cheese and other Andalusian *manjares* (delights). Perhaps we would pick an orange right from a tree and eat it together. The picnic had started out well enough; then the sun set, and the skittering and rustling around us became unmistakable. A battalion of rats was deploying. I lifted the four corners of the blanket, flung it over my shoulder like a Santa sack, and we fled.

My wife shuddered now, remembering it. "Which was the other one?"

"On that day trip to El Pedroso."

"Oh, right. You told me you wanted to see the Andalusian countryside, so I started taking you to the hill towns. You were always so silent on the drive back. I thought you were bored to death."

"No, just wiped out from speaking Spanish all day. Speaking a foreign language takes effort!"

"*¡Qué sufrío eres!*" (How long-suffering you are!)

"Hey, I loved those trips! On that one, we laid out our spread on a grassy slope, and you pulled out an orange for us to share. Remember what happened next?"

As I waited for her answer, she looked out over the countryside that she had spent so much of her childhood in. Her father had foraged for wild asparagus out there, and pine nuts that she and her sister would snack on with relish, and *tila* (lime blossoms) to calm her mother's nerves.

"Sorry, *cariño*," she said. "I don't."

"It was the way you peeled it, with a knife, using six simple cuts. First around the top, then around the bottom, then four slices along the sides, quartering it. You popped off the top and bottom with the dull edge of the knife, then peeled away the strips. Then the grand finale, sinking your thumbs into where the navel had been, and tearing away. *¡Mira por dónde!* (Lo and behold!) There was the fruit, split in half and ready to eat."

"Nothing special about that."

"Not to you maybe. But I'd hardly ever eaten oranges, or only as juice. They were such a pain to peel. I could never get my thumbs under the skin without breaking into the pulpy part. My hands would get all sticky. The pith would get caught under my fingernails. I'd end up just ripping the thing open, and juice would squirt everywhere. But you did it all so cleanly and effortlessly. Even when you split the orange open it didn't bleed. *Olé.*"

"*Pues, chiquillo, si fue eso lo que más te impresionó...*" (Well, kiddo, if that was what impressed you most...)

"'Better half,'" I said. "That's a more precise translation of 'half orange.' After we became a team, so much happened that I thought was beyond me. Nothing special, you say. But you knew what to do to make a full life seem a few simple steps away."

The Plato Lucio was set down before us: potatoes, eggs, and sausage—not exactly an exotic combination in the States, but here, like so much else, it seemed like a revelation.

AN APOLOGY FOR DREAMS

In my effort to perfect my Spanish, I struggled with the tiny words, especially the prepositions. For example, the English verb-preposition combination "to dream about" is translated to Spanish as *soñar con*, literally meaning "to dream with." When I mistakenly say, as I often do, *soñar sobre* (to dream about), I am speaking in Spanish but thinking in English. It should come as no surprise that a new language spoken correctly ends up reprogramming you.

In order to communicate "to dream with" in Spanish, you have to use *soñar juntos* (to dream together), which my half orange and I do not do, certainly not when we sleep.

My half orange has the most fascinating dreams. She'll be climbing a mountain in the fog, unsure why, yet still pulling herself up, foothold by handhold, utterly exhausted, until she reaches her physical limit. Just when she's sure she can't go on, a hand drops down from the mist, grabs onto her own, and she wakes up.

Or she'll be riding a rickety bicycle with loose and twisted handlebars and faulty brakes. With enormous effort, and avoiding one close call after another, she remains forever on the cusp of reaching some impossible destination.

Or she'll be on a high-speed train with the doors and windows wide open, whooshing through tunnels and over bridges, the only one in her car, yet unafraid. She is almost always alone in her dreams, except in one, where she was accompanied by a "*guapísimo*" (gorgeous) Afro-Cuban bouncer she was once acquainted with. I try not to analyze that dream too much. Whenever I make an appearance in her dreams, I am always flirting with some "*pelandrusca*" (floozy), and my wife is about to leave me.

I don't know if I have fascinating dreams, because I haven't remembered them in years. One day I asked her why she thought that was.

"Maybe because you exercise your subconscious enough when you write," she said.

Yes!

So perhaps we can say that, when I am scribbling away, my half orange and I *do* dream together. It's a joint effort. That reminds me of a line from *La Ciudad* (The City), in which the all-time greatest Sevillian journalist, Manuel Chaves Nogales, describes a female character this way:

"Es ella toda la espiritualidad sevillana, y una misión de cultura honda y honrada la recoge amorosamente, abre cauce sereno al caudal de su ánimo glorioso, y en él diluye, para que alcance a todas nuestras horas, aquel inapreciable tesoro de su emotividad."

That is, "she"—let's call her my half orange—"is Seville in its entirety, and a deep and honored cultural mission"—let's call that me—"lovingly takes her up, and opens a serene channel for her glorious and gushing spirit and the priceless treasure of her feelings to mingle with his and fill our every hour."

What dreamy words! In Spanish, "dreamy" translates to *onírico*. An English synonym for "dreamy" is "oneiric." Spanish taught me that.

Life with my half orange is discovery, always has been. We began living together four whirlwind months after we met. A month later, we stopped caring if our love-making resulted in a child. The next month, the child was conceived. Fourteen months after our first son was born, the second one furthered the revolution.

I became sleep-deprived, stopped reading, no longer took runs along the river. My time for writing was cut in half, and I found myself taking to the task with different priorities, the main one being to learn to defend and preserve myself in this new language and new world, while somehow adapting, too. Writing became my way to *darle vueltas a todo* (give everything turns), like you would a *tortilla* (Spanish omelet), so that the insides reached just the right savory consistency.

On the one hand, there was still the culture I had walked away from yet could not help but carry with me. On the other, there was the culture I had crashed and was now settled in, which could not help but form me, sometimes to my delight, other times to my dismay. But amidst all this mixing and clashing of cultures, one thing became increasingly clear—who and what I loved, namely, my half orange and the two wedges she has blessed me with.

Gajo, the Spanish word for the wedge of a citrus fruit, cannot be translated as love-child in the way that *media naranja* can be translated as soulmate. I only want to complete the metaphor. I like the image of children emerging outward from our center. Maybe it will mark their future in a happy way. I have discovered that words, when applied to what we love, can work like self-fulfilling prophecies.

Does a word express who or what we love, or is it the other way around—the people and things we love becoming more and more like the words or phrases we use to identify them? Since settling in Seville, I have noticed that sometimes only Spanish, or *andalú*, the Andalusian dialect, can precisely describe how I now see and make sense of the world. In English, the word "soulmate" does not work for my wife because it implies that we have always existed together on some ethereal plane, and I know nothing about the ethereal. I've said "better half" might be a more accurate translation, but that's got no juice to it, whereas the mere mention of *media naranja* has come to satisfy my thirst—sweet but not sugary, healthy, providing me with some essential nutrients that, before we met, I never knew I needed.

To be honest, I'm not sure if I fell in love with my half orange or Seville first. Perhaps it really was simultaneous. When our wedges came along, I loved them most deeply of all. Perhaps Seville has inspired me so because it is the only place where I have ever felt like a secondary character in my own story. As I straddled two worlds, soaking up and trying to assimilate anything that might help me sink in roots and hold my own, I found that everyday life with my family contained most of the necessary clues. Family became *familia*, which is different, lingering longer on the tongue.

Because I now consider my family the best part of who I have become, this book is a conversation with my adoptive land, with my homeland, with myself. Most of all it is a conversation with my half orange, more Sevillian than the Giraldillo, the 1.2-ton statue of a woman warrior, doubling as a weather vane, that crowns the twelfth-century bell tower of the Seville Cathedral.

It's supposed to represent faith. I imagine that for the wind to move a colossus like that, the whole cathedral would have to be blown down first.

TWISTED TONGUES

LEARN SPANISH IN YOUR CAR

After thirty-seven years in New York City, I arrived at my now adoptive city in November of 2005 in search of adventure, whatever that meant. I preferred to live in a place known more for the warmth of its people than for its competitiveness and cosmopolitanism, at least until I learned Spanish, which I thought would take a year, maybe two. Spanish would serve me well back in New York, a multilingual city if there ever was one. I had once taught a college writing class that included first-generation immigrants from eleven different countries!

What made me choose Seville over other Spanish-speaking places was a photo I saw on the internet of the rear façade of the Seville City Hall, a grand example of the *plateresco* (Plateresque) style, so named for its extensive and elaborate reliefs, sculpted as though molded in *plata* (silver). The reliefs ran from one end of the building to the other, or almost. A quarter of the façade was left undone, blank, untouched for more than forty years. One of the first busts carved into it, back in the fifteenth century, was Julius Caesar's, who granted Seville Roman-colony status in 45 B.C. One of the last was Grace Kelly's, who visited the city's famous April Fair in 1966, a year before I was born. I liked the idea of a prolonged visit to a city that didn't mind leaving a five-hundred-year project unfinished, perhaps forever, and which put the former Hollywood icon on equal footing with the conquering Roman emperor.

I had read up on the surrounding region, Andalusia. Its history was mind-boggling. Thanks to its temperate climate and the Guadalquivir River, which famously ran through Seville, as well as ports on both the Mediterranean and Atlantic coasts, Andalusia was already well-populated and civilized even before the Romans got there in about 200 B.C.

The intermixing of ancient cultures and creeds combined with the weather, the political folly, the aristocratic decadence, and the stubborn persistence of the poor to be happy and to live with dignity despite everything seeming to work against them had given the region a unique character and personality that lent itself to cliché. Flamenco, bullfighting, the siesta, the good-natured but cunning rogue, the women's Carmen-like beauty, the religious spectacle, the relentless sun, the ochre dust, the lime-covered houses, the land forgotten in time—in short, Spanish fatalism, apathy, idealism, resourcefulness, sensuality, and bravery—all of it seemed to have been either born or bred to perfection in Spain's southernmost and most populous *comunidad autónoma* (autonomous community), which was about the size of Maine or South Carolina and had just over 8.5 million people. Seville, the capital, with about 700,000 residents, was Spain's fourth largest city, behind Madrid, Barcelona, and Valencia.

So that was the history, geography, and demographics in a nutshell, but what about the language? That turned out to be trickier.

If you consider yourself capable of becoming fluent in another language in less than two years, without immersing yourself in it twenty-four hours a day, either you live in dreamland or you're a genius. These quick and easy language-learning programs that advertise themselves only want your money. After you spend forty hours, or even six months, on a course, perhaps on the internet, and you earn a certificate qualifying you at some upper level, you're still just a beginner, taking baby steps. Even if you go the traditional route, spending one hundred fifty or two hundred hours of quality class time in a legitimate language academy, do not expect too much. You can learn a language in an academy just like you can learn to dance flamenco in an academy. It's a mere introduction, so you can start to understand the difficulty of it.

I began to learn Spanish in July of 2005. I was still in New York, with six months left before my Teaching English as a Foreign Language (TEFL) course began in Seville. I bought *Learn Spanish in Your Car*, a packet with three CDs and an accompanying booklet.

I passed meticulously through the lessons one by one, never missing a day. I made cards with new vocabulary, hundreds and hundreds of words and phrases, and pulled them out of their boxes at random in my free time, wanting to be sufficiently prepared. Days before leaving for Seville, I had qualified as "advanced." How proud I felt! As I took my seat on the bus that would take me to the airport, I saw the sticker on the window, *salida de emergencia* (emergency exit), and did not even have to think to understand it.

No fear, I thought. You've done your homework.

When I arrived at my destination fifteen hours later, I remembered those now taunting words and wished I had bailed out when I still had the chance. The only words I heard in the avalanche of new sounds that assaulted my ears were *vale* and *venga*, which had been covered on my CDs as, respectively, the third-person form of *valer*, meaning "to be worth," and the third-person imperative of *venir*, meaning "to come." But that wasn't the half of it, not even close.

Picture me recently arrived in the Seville airport, stomach growling from hunger, trying to buy a sandwich. The woman at the counter says, "*Vale cinco euros, ¿vale?*" (It's worth five euros, worth?) and then, when she sees my ten-dollar bill, adds, "*Lo siento, ese no vale.*" (I'm sorry, that isn't worth.) Turned out that *valer* not only meant "to be worth," but also "to cost," "to be understood," and "to be acceptable."

Venga was no less multipurpose. In addition to expressing "come" as a command, it could also mean, "Okay, agreed" (sort of like *vale*). Again, picture me, still a neophyte in everything Spanish and Sevillian, stopping at an office to ask if I could leave a resumé. The receptionist said, "*Venga,*" and held out a hand, meaning she would take my resumé, but I understood that I should accompany her, that she would lead me to the head of personnel by the hand.

What good did studying grammar, structure, and vocabulary do if there were a different set of rules in real life?

So much preparation, and it turned out I knew nothing.

Weeks passed and nothing changed. The situation actually got worse because I lost my self-confidence. When it comes to speaking a foreign language, if you doubt yourself, you're doomed. On my first day of work, I was greeted by the security guard of the industrial park where I would be teaching English to a group of internationally-minded business folk.

"*Buenos días,*" (Good morning,) he said.

I heard, "*Podía.*" (You could.)

"*¿Podía qué?*" (I could what?) I said.

"*¿Cómo?*" Literally "How?"—as in "How's that?"—but that's not what I understood.

"*¿Cómo podía qué?*" (How could I do what?) I said.

He looked at me like it was way too early for Abbott and Costello routines. "*¿De qué me está hablando usted?*" (What are you talking about?)

All I heard was *blando* (soft) and *usted* (you), and thought he was calling me soft in the head.

And that's how I felt. I lived constantly on the defensive. I remember a guy stopping me once to ask directions for Santa Justa, Seville's train station. When I told him I didn't know, he shook his head and said, "*¿Tú tampoco, eh?*" (You neither, huh?)

What I understood was "*Tú eres tan poco*" (You are so small) for not being able to help him. Thank God I didn't know enough Spanish to respond in kind to the imagined insult.

Meeting my half orange revolutionized my Spanish. From the very beginning, we spoke in her native tongue—reluctantly on her part because she wanted to learn English almost as badly as I wanted to learn Spanish. I remember the conversation in which we decided that my Spanish took priority, or rather I decided it.

"Look," I said. "This is my moment. If we ever go live in the United States, that'll be your moment, okay?"

Selfish, yes, but I had changed my life to come to Spain and was damned if I was going to teach English on my personal time as well.

My half orange is beautiful, has the patience to watch grass grow, and was in love with me. Ideal qualities in a teacher. Thanks to her, I reached the milestone of being able to understand the spoken language better than I could explain myself in it. That's when I began to experience the biggest drag of learning a foreign language abroad, or at least of learning Spanish in Seville: the natives began trying to finish my sentences. As I paused to correctly form what I wanted to say, they would fall over themselves trying to guess it first. Their intention was probably to save me trouble, but I felt like the host of a game show struggling to keep a bunch of overly eager contestants from jumping the gun. I actually preferred the days when they used to gesticulate and shout in my face, as though I were hard of hearing.

Long after moving in with my half orange and speaking Spanish at home, the struggle to understand others and explain myself continued. For example, my mother-in-law's way of speaking would forever leave me perplexed. In defense of her grandson when I scolded him, she would say things like, "*No relates al chiquillo,*" (Don't recount to the kid,) or "*No hay que darle traquíos.*" (You don't have to give him booms.) The first time she laid eyes on him, she said, "*¡Qué bien despachao!*" (How well dispatched!) When hungry, she would claim to be "*esmayao,*" which, if it had a "d" at the beginning and another between the "a" and the "o" at the end, would have meant "faint." When tired, she would be "*abriendo mucho la boca,*" (opening the mouth a lot,) which apparently meant to yawn. If my father-in-law was in a foul mood, she would say to him, "*¡Anda que no tienes un fú!*" (Walk that you don't have a fury!) And most confusing of all, she would address me as "*niño*" (boy) and my sons as "*padre*" (father)—lingo that, according to my wife, was "*de pueblo*" (of town).

I was still far from fluent when Wedge One was born in 2008. In the hospital, the doctors were speaking two foreign languages as far as I was concerned. If you are a native speaker and doctors fall into their infuriating jargon, at least then you know that your confusion is the doctor's fault for failing to translate the medical vernacular into something that patients or their loved ones can reasonably be expected to understand. We foreigners, on the other hand, cannot know if the problem lies with our inadequate language skills or the doctor's poor bedside manner. After Wedge One was born, he had to be kept in an incubator for three days because of low blood sugar. I found out the reason only because my wife told me. Not once did I have a clue what the doctors were saying.

When the three of us left that hospital, I gave thanks to God and swore to put mastering Spanish ahead of everything except my new family. Clearly, I needed it to take care of them. I needed it to make myself *valer* (be understood, acceptable, worthy).

NO NOT EVEN NOTHING

As if *andalú*, the Andalusian dialect, weren't enough to frustrate me when it came to communication, there was the locals' very singular habit of saying the literal opposite of what they really meant.

I would learn the hard way that if a comment began with *"Anda que..."* (Walk that...), it meant talk was about to take an ironic turn.

Like the time a neighbor, referring to a butcher's shop in the neighborhood of Nervión, said to me, *"¡Anda que no es cara!"* (Walk that it's not expensive!) Taking the commentary at face value, I stopped in to buy a pork tenderloin the next time I found myself passing by said shop. After paying almost double what I would have paid in the supermarket, I thought, *Why on earth does my neighbor want to mislead me?*

Another day when I was waiting with the wedges for the elevator on our way out of the building, the doors opened and a neighbor emerged, having come up from the street.

"¡Anda que no hace frío ni ná!" (Walk that it's not cold out, not even nothing!) he said.

Once again, interpreting the words literally, I removed various layers of clothing from my boys as the elevator dropped to the ground floor. When we stepped out the front door and the first gust of stiff, cold wind hit us in the face, I asked myself, "How in God's name have I lived in Seville for five years and still can't understand the natives when they talk about the weather?"

While my neighbors confused me with their linguistic idiosyncrasies, I confused them with, well, *me*.

"¡Anda que el crío no va a gusto!" (Walk that the kid doesn't go comfortable!) exclaimed a neighbor when she ran into me in the street one day as I carried Wedge One, still only months old, mounted on my chest in a sling.

The old women in my building were generally traditionalist to a fault, believing that a man alone with a baby was an accident waiting to happen. This added to my miscomprehension because I was expecting disapproval. My half orange liked to say that I *"andaba"* (walked, yes) among these women *"con la escopeta siempre cargá"* (with the shotgun always loaded). Well, at this woman, I fired. She had only wanted to make a passing comment, but I stopped square in front of her with my son strapped to me like a bulletproof vest. I shook my head in emphatic disagreement, saying that she was terribly mistaken, that my son's head was extremely well supported, that German engineers designed these contraptions, and that pediatricians had shown, and personal experience had confirmed, that being carried around in an upright position did wonders for gas expulsion.

She looked at me as if I were exactly what I was: a poor, lost *guiri*.

The first time I managed to communicate the exact opposite of the literal significance of my words, I did it by accident. Very often, when I would speak my adoptive tongue in those years, the words would get caught in my throat, resulting in an "ankh!" sound. Turned out that "ankh" sounded a lot like *"Anda que…"*.

One day, a woman in the street managed to get a smile out of Wedge One, and I wanted to explain to her that this was by no means a common occurrence.

"Ankh, he doesn't smile a lot in the street," I said.

The woman bent down, putting her beaming ancient face over my son's beaming brand new one.

"¿Chíí?" (Ooo yeeeah?) she said. *"¿Eres tú muy chimpático, verdad?"* (Yew a vewwy happy baby, arwwe yew?)

"Ankh, no," I said.

"¡A que chí!" (Yes, yew arwwe!) she said, tickling his chin. *"¡Papá dice que chí!"* (Daddy says you arwwe!)

I wanted the woman to understand that I was paying her a compliment.

"Ankh... no... common... you," I managed to say, before my mind went blank and my throat became too dry and taut to even ankh again.

Back home, I turned to my half orange for consolation.

"Do you think I get overanxious when I have to speak Spanish to strangers?" I asked.

"*No ni ná*," (No not even nothing,) she said.

Misunderstanding her, I felt reassured.

Because I was almost always straining and flailing in the native language, or at least a beat behind, when I would spot someone wearing a T-shirt in English, it felt like a chance encounter with an old friend, no matter what the T-shirt said. These encounters were also a subtle form of settling the score, or at least of temporarily turning the tables. For example, one day I saw a neighborhood kid wearing a T-shirt that said "Over my head," and I could not help but feel a pang of smug satisfaction that among the things over this kid's head were probably the words written across his chest.

Personally, I have never needed a T-shirt to call attention to my ridiculousness. At least not in Spain. I've only had to speak and to fail to understand. However, a phrase has occurred to me, which, if I wore it on a T-shirt, might serve as a response to any and all Sevillians who want to direct a question to me in their native tongue: *Pregúntale a mi mujer* (Ask my wife).

Walk that she hasn't gotten me out of jams. Like that time with the pears.

But you know what's funny? My mother also sometimes says the opposite of what she really means, and my half orange can't make sense of it. Granted, the Sevillian switcheroo is a manner of speaking, while my mom is just being overly prudent, but still.

"Look," I said to my wife. "When my mother says that the grapes are a little bitter or that the cake is a little dry, what she really wants to say is that she hopes you think the grapes are sweet and that the cake is baked just right."

"Well, when she talks like that, I don't feel like trying them," my half orange replied.

"How is that possible?" I said. "One of your fellow Sevillians might say, 'The grapes aren't in their point, not nothing' or 'Walk that the cake isn't of sucking the fingers!' Apply the same semantic logic that's applied in your city, and you'll understand my mother perfectly."

Sarcasm like, "Oh, that was a smooth move," or "Fantastic restaurant you picked, genius," which also means the opposite of the words' literal sense, has always rubbed me wrong, but Sevillians' linguistic ironies are so ingrained and widespread that I cannot use them to draw conclusions about the personalities of the people who employ them, because everybody employs them.

For years, I could only draw conclusions about myself—that I was still a baby in my second language, and that maybe if someone carried me around in a sling, people might understand me from the sounds that emerged from my opposite end.

COÑO

Wedge One, at twenty-two months old, scooted under the coffee table in my in-laws' living room and refused to come out.

"*No hay coño de sacarlo,*" (Not a *cunnus*—without *lingus* [wink, wink]—exists to get him out of there,) exclaimed my mother-in-law, the same woman who can't say "See you tomorrow" without adding "*si Dios quiere*" (God willing), whose idea of a good film features former child star Joselito singing to sheep, and who has a homemade sanctuary in her living room dedicated to local luminary Saint Angela of the Cross.

I returned home with María's phrase still ringing in my ears and expressed my bewilderment to my wife.

"I imagined a contest," I said. "A line of women approaching the coffee table, lifting their skirts one by one, hoping their *coño* might be the one to entice him out."

My half orange laughed in my face.

"It's just a manner of speaking," she said.

"Right," I said. "More or less like the other day when Wedge Two shot a stream of urine on your blouse and you screamed out, '*Me cago en tu padre*' (I shit on your father), who happens to be me, in case you hadn't noticed."

"*Qué hombre,*" (What a man,) she said. "*Siempre tomando las cosas al pie de la letra.*" (Always taking the things to the foot of the letter.)

It was true. I could not help understanding Sevillians literally. A guy in my building would respond to my son's standoffishness by saying, "*El jodido por culo, este. Qué escrupuloso es.*" (The screwed-in-the-ass, this one. How squeamish he is.) Even though he said it in the most affectionate tone possible, my ears still burned.

As a teacher of English as a second language, I understood that vulgarity was tricky. When wannabe hotshot students would trot out all the tough-guy talk they had picked up from *Grand Theft Auto* and original language versions of Scorsese and Tarantino films, I didn't even bother correcting them. "You are fucking me!" I would hear, and knew the kid meant, "You are fucking *with* me." Or "This weather is a shit," a student might say when it rained. It was hopeless to explain. Just think of all the things "shit" can express in the United States—surprise, joy, rage, awe—depending on context and tone, not to mention that it can have the exact opposite meaning if the article in front of it changes from definite ("You are the shit") to indefinite ("You are a shit"). And shouldn't "give a shit" and "take a shit" swap meanings? Unless my students lived abroad for a few years, soaking up all the nuances, they would almost always look ridiculous when using expletives.

As would I if I ever tried to blow off steam with the Sevillian variety. For years I mixed up the phrases *hijo de la gran puta* (son of the great whore) and *puta madre* (mother whore). Just like "a shit" and "the shit," they express the exact opposite. When your soccer team scores a sensational goal, you say "mother whore." But when you find out that an offside call has nullified that goal, you say, "Son of the great whore." In a house of prostitution, couldn't the great whore be the same as the mother whore? Because of that thought, I kept confusing the two phrases. If I dared to use vulgarity to express disgust or delight in Spanish, a hybrid of the two phrases would emerge, something like "Son of the mother whore." The equivalent in English might be "Mother bitcher."

I once considered hip-hop cutting-edge for how it used foul language to express tenderness. When the rapper Method Man, playing the role of prisoner in the track "All I Need," appealed to his ghetto sweetheart with, "Never ever give my pussy away and keep it tight, aiight?" it sounded to me like an aching plea for fidelity. Then I settled in Seville and saw that little old ladies were pulling off this stunt on a regular basis, and probably had been for centuries before the United States even existed.

"*¿Qué pasa, churrita?*" (What's happening, weenie?) Isabel from next door would casually ask Wedge One. If the little guy then did something adorable, we might hear, "*Que te como los huevitos.*" (I eat your little balls.)

But the free and almost ubiquitous use of *coño* was the most difficult thing for me to assimilate. *Coño* is harsh (although not as harsh as "cunt"). No matter how often I heard it emerging from the mouths of grandmothers, children, teachers, and even priests, my ear refused to become desensitized. I was aware that nine out of ten times the Sevillians used it to communicate their signature irony or to emphasize a point, not even thinking about the object it was referring to. Even so, for years the word came across to me *en carne viva* (in living meat), meaning raw.

It assaulted me from every corner of the city. A young waitress in a café said to her co-worker, "*¡Me encanta, coño!*" (I love it, *coño*!), and I understood the phrase without the comma, "*¡Me encanta coño!*" (I love *coño*!), causing me to blush. While we English speakers sometimes respond to a preposterous comment by saying, "My ass!", Sevillians will say, "*El coño de tu hermana.*" (Your sister's *coño*.) I'd fight not to imagine it, minding its own business three thousand miles away. Or take the Sevillian wrinkle on *en el quinto pino* (in the fifth pine), meaning "in the boonies." An otherwise distinguished lady once entered my class and explained her lateness by saying, "*Aparqué en el quinto coño.*" (I parked in the fifth *coño*.) I stood at the blackboard with chalk in hand, picturing five *coños* big enough to have clearance.

Or how many Sevillians, after taking the liberty to pick one of my boys up off the ground, have bellowed out, "*¡Qué bonito eres, coño!*" (How beautiful you are, *coño*!)?

"Son of the mother whore!" I'd want to scream.

I guess my point is that even when we know the meaning of a word, that doesn't mean we understand it, much less how to use it.

Once at a party, I went to the kitchen to get a beer from the fridge and found the host there getting one for himself. He looked at me with that snide Sevillian irony and addressed me with his city's equivalent of "What the [expletive] do you want?"—"*¿Qué coño quieres?*" Literally, "What *coño* do you want?"

"My wife's, thank you very much," I said.

He didn't get the joke even after I tried to explain it.

FIELD WORK

The tendency among young Sevillians to wear T-shirts with English phrases on them—phrases I suspected they misunderstood—continued to provide me with food for thought. English projected a hip international image and style that young people no doubt wanted to make their own, but most of them seemed drawn to English as someone might be drawn to a song for its melody, regardless of the lyrics. But the lyrics, like that old friend calling out to me, could not be ignored.

One day it occurred to me that there might be an entertaining English lesson in all this, and I began to collect tag lines off the T-shirts I encountered in the street. Most of the heavy investigative work took place during the hot months when there was less to block my view of the primary source, which in many cases was plastered across the chests of statuesque young women.

"Occupational hazards," I explained to my half orange. "We English teachers gotta live dangerously."

I carried a notepad around with me. "I liked being a go-go dancer" was one of the first choice nuggets I jotted down. Perhaps the wearer thought it meant, "I like to go dancing"? Then I came across, "Fancy a ride?" also worn by a nubile young lady, and then, "Stand under my umbrella." In this instance, the power of the message was communicated more by context, or rather by the chest that offered said refuge, ample enough to keep at least one lucky guy out of the rain. The less subtle but by no means hyperbolic "INCREDIBLE" appeared a few days later stretched across the rack of another eye-opening object of my research.

One weekend, my half orange and I were moseying through the local mall, taking turns pushing the double stroller. I pointed out a bold assertion that bobbed past, buxomly borne: "I like your boyfriend," which reminded me of a couple of others that I'd recently noted down: "Friend with benefits" and "I'm great in bed."

"Would these girls parade around in public with these pronouncements across their chests if they were written in Spanish?" I asked.

She shrugged her shoulders, showing very little interest.

I spied more brash language, worn by a young man for a change. "Keep your hands to yourself," it said.

"That's the battle cry these young women should be wearing!" I said.

My moralizing wasn't convincing her, so I tried humor.

"What these young women need is a concerned and attentive English professor to teach them all the nuances of the Anglo-Saxon tongue."

Even my comedy left her cold.

The T-shirts and their slogans pursued me relentlessly, all worn by tall, dewy drinks of water: "Do you think you can trust me?" "I like boys with bad habits," "Don't leave me alone." I was fast approaching sensory overload, and so appealed to my half orange one last time.

"Surely many of these young women dream of long-lasting love and would like to have a family one day? Why are they wearing T-shirts that undermine what they most likely base their future happiness on?"

"Why do you insist on taking the words so literally?"

"Is it too much to ask that they consult a Spanish-English dictionary before buying their clothes?"

Another Sevillian pleasure skiff passed, plying my turbulent waters with the words printed across her prow: "The naked truth about the dark places."

"See!" I said. "I'm being provoked!"

My half orange stopped and bent over Wedge Two, adjusting his blanket so he would not get a chill from the frigid commercial center air. She straightened up, her brow creased in thought, peering off into the distance.

"What?" I said.

"Nothing," she said. "I'm just imagining a buff twenty-year-old with a message written across the fly of his pants, 'I am a stallion. You will not regret it,' or 'Up to the hilt.'"

She moved aside so I could push the stroller for a while.

"I definitely see what you mean," she said, taking away my notepad. "The suggestive power of words."

Class dismissed.

THE GENDER GURU

After thirty-six years of speaking only English, I suddenly found myself immersed in a language that classifies each noun—the most basic and practical element of language—as either masculine or feminine. Languages are supposed to be wise and to give us answers. If cultural forces made *casa*, the most common Spanish word for "home," feminine, and its more stilted synonym, *hogar*, masculine, that has to tell us something, right?

In English, of course, nouns are gender neutral. They have no agreed upon association with masculine or feminine, except with words like "man" or "woman," "rooster" or "hen," and sometimes with gender-specific job titles like "waiter" and "waitress." In Spanish, too, such words correspond to their logical grammatical gender. But many of the rest of the nouns in Spanish are enough to spark convoluted debates in me, as I rack my brain for hidden clues on how gender affects human behavior.

When searching for the right word in Spanish, I often wind up wondering about the gender, especially if I don't remember it. And I have to remember it if I want to speak correctly, because Spanish is a language in which the articles, some pronouns, and almost all adjectives change to agree with the gender of the nouns.

Sometimes the grammatical gender of the Spanish nouns and my personal understanding of gender go hand in hand: *día* (day) is masculine, *noche* (night) is feminine; *camino* (way or path) is masculine, *costumbre* (habit or tradition) feminine; *conocimiento* (knowledge) is masculine, *sabiduría* (wisdom) feminine. On occasion, the meaning of the Spanish word changes depending on the gender assigned to it: *orden* (order) is masculine when it refers to "arrangement," but feminine when it refers to "command." I'm not sure I concur there. And what about the fact that *paraíso* (paradise) is masculine, but *muerte* (death) feminine? Does it make sense that *amor* (love), *cariño* (affection), and *beso* (kiss) are masculine, and *cárcel* (prison), *guerra* (war), and *bala* (bullet) feminine? How did *cotilleo* (gossip) become masculine and *fanfarronería* (bravado) feminine? Or *lógica* (logic) feminine and *presentimiento* (premonition) masculine? Did the inventors of the language assign gender to certain words, hoping to have a joke at future speakers' expense, or does my confusion just put all my sexist prejudices and stereotypes on glaring display?

I know there are rules to help me figure out the gender of Spanish nouns. For example, the endings *"ción"* and *"a"* usually indicate feminine nouns, while *"ón"* and *"o"* indicate masculine ones. But then there are the exceptions. Although *problema* (problem) ends in *"a,"* the word has been categorized as masculine because the suffix *"ema"* derives from Greek. On the other hand, you have *mano* (hand), which ends in *"o"* but is feminine. Apparently the reasons for that association have to do with Latin. So Greek conventions dictate in some cases and Latin conventions in others. For what reason? Instead of satisfying me, the explanations only serve to further complicate the issue.

I don't agree with the linguists who consider the gender of nouns a grammatical accident. I believe that the words and rules of the language evolved together, organically, and had more to do with poetry and human instinct than chance or cold linguistic logic. There are reasons for the gender given to each Spanish noun, just not clear ones, and I am out to find the sense in them.

Here's an example of how my mind flies off. Take the words *resultado* (outcome) and *idea* (idea). Did *resultado* end up masculine because men are usually more headstrong than women when it comes to getting to the end of a task, and *idea* turn out feminine because women are usually more open to considering different ways of doing things? Or did the gender of these nouns have more to do with the fact that *resultado* brings to mind an arrow stuck in a target, something phallic, while *idea* evokes more the target itself, hypnotizing, *casa*-like, inviting our arrows toward it? My ruminations can go on like that, without end. Let's not even talk about the wanderings of my mind when I discovered that although *pene* (penis) is gender masculine and *vagina* (vagina) gender feminine, things are not so straightforward when speaking colloquially or vulgarly. *Churrina* and *polla*, meaning "wienie" and "dick," are feminine, and *chocho* and *coño*, meaning you-know-what, are masculine. Go figure.

Before learning Spanish, when I heard or saw the word "hand," perhaps certain subconscious gender associations were tied to it, but none were imposed by the grammar. Now, because *mano* is oddly feminine (that "*o*" should make it masculine), the meaning of the word has expanded and therefore changed; it has become more defined, richer. If Spanish had been my first language, would I have associated "hand" with the feminine long before most of the other associations could come into play? "Hand" has huge metaphoric power. Would seeing it differently from the start have changed my life in some vital way? I know that most native Spanish speakers have assimilated grammatical gender to the point that they do not even think about it, but does that mean that they have unthinkingly assimilated the associations, too?

Could it be that, deep in the Spanish subconscious, a hand is sleek, dexterous, and affectionate, hanging limply off the wrist? Because *arte* (art) is masculine in singular and feminine in plural, were Spanish speakers less surprised than English speakers by the lusty films of a young and androgynous Almodóvar? Is the gender ambiguity of *arte* also the reason why Spaniards generally see Hemingway, smiling robustly behind his beard, as exotic and can relate more to the flamboyant genius of Oscar Wilde?

Or take the problematic *problema*, for the errors it regularly provokes in those learning Spanish. For me, the correct masculine definite article—*el problema* rather than *la problema*—finally clicked only after I had spent enough time with my future wife to realize that most of my previous *problemas* in romantic relationships had less to do with the women than with me and my ideas about what it meant to be a man.

The Real Academia Española (RAE), or Spanish Royal Academy, is the governmental body that watches over the language's "essential unity" by writing the country's official dictionaries and manuals of grammar, spelling, and usage. *Limpia, fija y da splendor* (Clean, steadfast, and giving splendor) is its motto—perhaps a bit too steadfast, because a few years ago it angered Spanish feminists by refusing to concede that *médico* (doctor) and *miembro* (member, for example, of a club) could have their endings changed from "*o*" to "*a*" when referring to a woman.

Compounding the controversy, only eleven of the RAE's almost five hundred *miembros* have been women since the institution was founded in 1713. Even so, I think feminists have bigger fish to fry. The language has been good to women by making *historia* (history), *gente* (people), and *razón* (the state of being right) feminine, but what about linguistic atrocities like *embarazo* (pregnancy) and *parto* (birth) being masculine? As far as revolutionary changes go, why not a movement to make *mierda* (shit) and *brutalidad* (brutality) masculine, and *valor* (value) and *sol* (sun) feminine?

Personally, although I see some discrepancies in how gender has been assigned to words, I would not change a thing about the Spanish language. I like that certain aspects of it remain as unalterable and mysterious as the universe. Astrologists look for answers in the stars; I look for them in the gender of Spanish nouns. There have to be illuminating reasons why *plazo* (deadline) got that masculine "*o*" while *plaza* (city square) that feminine "*a*," why *esfuerzo* (effort) got the "*o*" and *fuerza* (strength) the "*a*." Is a *puerto* (port) somehow more masculine than a *puerta* (door)? In what way?

The answer could constitute a *problema* all its own. Every Spanish translation of "answer"—*respuesta* (response), *réplica* (reply), *reacción* (reaction), *solución* (solution), *resolución* (resolution), *contestación* (contestation)—is feminine, except for *resultado* (result), mentioned above, and *escape* (escape).

"Why?" I asked my wife.

"*Porque sí*," (Just because,) she said.

Fair enough.

GETTING THROUGH

Supermarkets are as depressing in Seville as they are in the States—the soulless light, the morgue-like cold, the shopping carts piled high with the crap that people buy. I prefer mom-and-pop shops, where I can support a family enterprise while making conversation and sometimes even friends.

Upon settling into my half orange's apartment as a stay-at-home dad while she worked from nine to two, I soon discovered that one of the joys of living in Seville was that I could do all our shopping within a five-block radius drawn from our building's front door. The staples, however, were cheaper in the multinationals, and since the staples added up, I would take the car to the nearest megastore, Alcampo, once a week. Accompanied by the wedges, I normally went early on a weekday morning to beat the rush. On a good day, by the time we dropped back down to the underground parking, almost everybody else would just be getting there, and I would feel like I had stolen a march on the day.

Of course, things did not always go so smoothly. One day, because I had been waylaid by work and other annoying administrative tasks, I let the kids sleep an hour later. The shopping list was especially long that week and filled with items I didn't usually buy, which meant they took more time to find.

The wedges, as usual, had started out in the shopping cart, but, as it slowly filled, I had lifted them out. Then they ran up and down the aisles, disappearing around corners, and reappearing with stuff not on the list. After I sent them to put the stuff back, they would return with other, different stuff I didn't want to buy.

By the time we got to the checkout line, all three of us were itching to get out of there.

The best part of our routine was coming up. As a reward for a job well done, we would stop by the pet store on the ground floor to see the puppies sleeping or playing in their storefront pens, or to take in the racket of the birds, or to ponder the solemnity of the lizards, turtles, and fishes in their tanks.

Then we would head down to the parking garage. After unloading our cart and returning it to get the coin out of the deposit slot, we would play "Daddy Dropped His Change." I would pretend to accidentally drop the coin, and then all three of us would fight and scramble for it on the parking garage floor. That way we'd blow off some steam and get some exercise in.

But it turned out that the fun would have to wait. After we finished with the cashier, I checked the receipt and saw I had not received the discount I had expected on some bananas I thought I'd bought on sale. Only at Information could I return the fruit or have the price explained.

I dreaded such conversations, even more so in Spanish, which was exactly why I had to go through with it—to overcome my fears.

At that point the crowds had caught up to us. Every time I looked back on the way to Information, my wedges would be further behind, dragging their feet. People pushing carts or pulling trollies spilled off the escalators, then weaved in front of or around my sons.

"Get a move on, guys," I yelled.

They pointed downstairs.

"Not yet," I said. "One more thing."

They stopped and held their ground. Who could blame them?

Of course, anyone sensible would have thought, "To hell with saving a buck-fifty on a bunch of bananas. To the pet store!" but I just don't work that way. The more potentially frustrating and tedious the task before me, the more headstrong I am about getting it over with. I had to go to returns and get this sorted out so I could go home feeling satisfied with myself.

"If you two don't get over here right now," I shouted, "there'll be no pet store at all."

It worked, although having been unreasonable only wore at my patience even more.

Fortunately, the line at returns was not too long, although once I took my place, a half dozen people joined behind me. The boys ran back and forth along the commercial center's main thoroughfare. I would call them over to my side, but then I'd get distracted with the receipt again, trying to make sense of it, trying to recall all the Spanish vocabulary I would need to best express myself, and the boys would break free again.

Finally, it was my turn and I stepped up to the counter, showing the attendant my receipt. She nodded as I began my semi-prepared spiel and remained attentive until I brought it to a clumsy close. Then she pointed to where on the receipt the discount on the bananas appeared, next to some special code.

"Okay," I said, but since I had also bought other discounted fruit and vegetables, I wanted to be clear about which discounts were for what.

Math happens to be the last thing a language learner is able to do in a non-native tongue, and I was still far from clearing the final hurdles on the course. I had to translate numbers into English before I could do any kind of real math in my head, and this woman was throwing lots of figures at me while doing the calculations out loud, and I just wasn't able to keep up.

I asked her to run through the numbers once more, slowly.

"*Sin problema. Por supuesto,*" (No problem. Of course,) she said, and began again, going step by step. I was just starting to catch on when we were interrupted.

"*¡Aquí estamos esperando!*" (Here we are waiting!) someone said from the rear of the line, then added, "*¡Lo que uno tiene que aguantá!*" (What one has to put up with!)

I looked down the line at my heckler—tracksuit, slicked-back hair, two-day stubble, pouty-lipped sneer. When I met his eyes, he shook his head with smug disgust, clearly thinking he had spoken for the majority. This was exactly the type of situation that I dreaded as a *guiri*—my foreignness getting in people's way—but having some jerk finally point out my obstructiveness turned out to be a relief. Now I just had to deal with *him*. I turned around to look for the wedges, letting everyone know where my priorities lay. They were climbing on some coin-operated kiddie rides about fifty feet away. I turned back to the woman, who made a dismissive gesture in the direction of the heckler and continued her explanation.

I only pretended to listen, nodding along, buying time as I planned my big move.

Self-consciousness, the biggest foil to language learning, had miraculously disappeared, trumped by the desire to set the record straight.

When the woman finished talking, I thanked her for clearing things up, and then I about-faced without stepping away from the counter just yet. I called to my boys in English, the language I always used with them, but loudly now, for all to hear. Fathers alone with their sons in Sevillian supermarkets were just not a common sight—even less so during the week, when most kids the wedges' age were in day care or preschool. I wore Birkenstocks with white socks and cargo shorts, fitting the description of the tag I knew everybody in sight wanted to put on me. My hair was long and graying, my features angular. There was absolutely no way anybody could have mistaken me for anything but what I was—*not from there.*

But I was about to do something that would make that irrelevant.

From my tone of voice, the wedges sensed that something was up. They quickly climbed down off the kiddie rides and ran to me—a nice detail, a show of authority with my little ones, before I really brought the hammer down. When they sidled up to me, I put my arms around them and gently guided them to where my heckler stood. The line was almost all middle-aged and older women, except for my target, who, when he saw me coming, straightened up from his elbow-on-the-counter slouch and puffed out his chest, looking at us out of the corner of his eye.

A silence seemed to descend on the scene as I dropped to a knee, as though about to ask for his hand. In a way, we *would* soon be paired for eternity after this. With one arm still around each of my sweet citric sidekicks, I made eye contact first with Wedge One, then with Wedge Two, to let them and my captive audience know that I was about to impart a priceless lesson that would make things right with the world, at least this small part of it, for the moment.

I pointed to the man but still looked at and spoke to my sons, as loud as before, because I wanted to project.

"That man is rude, because he shouted at me when I didn't understand, although I was trying my best," I said. "Do not be like him, ever. And if I ever shout at you because you don't understand, even though you're trying your best, remind me of this man, and tell me I'm acting like him, because that will make me ashamed and stop what I'm doing."

After a stunned silence, a few women in the line nodded emphatically. One even clapped. My heckler stayed where he was, jiggling his leg in his sweatpants, drumming his fingers on the countertop, staring straight ahead, as if by ignoring me I would leave.

I got to my feet and backed away, keeping an eye on him, while herding my kids over to our shopping cart. A security guard had drifted over to investigate the commotion that my spontaneous theatre had stirred up. Clearly it was time to head for the escalator.

"Why did you speak Spanish to us?" Wedge One asked as we were carried downstairs. Wedge Two, his mind already on the pet store, was poised for the escalator to hit bottom so he could launch himself in a sprint to the storefront display.

I hadn't even thought about the language. It had been like speaking in a dream. I'd finally gotten through, in a language not my own.

EN PAZ

The solution in any language, I suspect, is to live in peace with the imprecision of communication. After all, stumbling over foreign words and expressions, misusing and misinterpreting them, is just an extreme case of what happens in our mother tongue. The problem is not so much the language, but rather people, and the abyss that yawns between us.

Take the day I brought my kids down to the park behind our building and said to a mother holding her baby, "Very cheerful, no?"

"No," she said. "He doesn't have teeth."

"But he's very *cheerful*, right?" I said, articulating *sonriente* (cheerful) as best I could. Somehow articulating always made things worse.

She shook her head and looked at her child's mouth, just to make sure.

"No," she repeated. "He doesn't have teeth."

I tried to take our failure of communication in stride, but, as my half orange liked to say, my transparency *me puso en evidencia* (put me on display). The woman moved away nervously, probably asking herself why this *guiri* was so furious that her son had no *dientes* (teeth).

I retreated to the refuge of my wedges. When they didn't understand me, at least I could blame it on *their* ignorance.

Later my half orange told me that if I had used the slightly more common word *risueño* (mirthful), the woman might have understood me. I doubted it. *Risueño* sounded a lot like *sueño* (sleep), at least when I said it.

People often put their own particular slant on what they hear. We send words out into the world, our intentions get lost, and the meaning is up for grabs—a smorgasbord of possible interpretations, no matter the nutritive benefits.

Which is a shame, because the nuances of language give insight into elusive but important ideas. Take, for instance, the phrases "in peace" and "at peace." I can be at peace with my surroundings, or in peace with them, but I prefer the second. To me, "at peace" means I have only just arrived and the peace might slip away at any moment, while "in peace" means I have entered, am already inside. In Spanish, *en paz* (in peace) is the only option. In peace with my surroundings, with those I live among, with the people I love, and of course with the languages I communicate and miscommunicate in. So, in Spanish, the perspective imposed by the language happens to be true for me—*en paz*. That's what I am here.

Spanish had already taught me something else about peace: that it doesn't have to mean being left alone; it might even mean the opposite. I discovered peace by throwing myself into the mix, by trying to understand and be understood. The confusion is just part of the fun.

Smiling... teeth... mirthful... sleep...

Read together, those four words sound like a poem.

A FEAST FOR THE SENSES

EL OÍDO

Only the midday summer heat keeps Seville silent, and never completely. There is always the muffled hum of the air conditioning units blowing hot air into the already scorching streets, and a purring undercurrent, like a dragon dozing, recharging its fire-breathing powers for when it's time to rear its head and raise Cain. Sevillians don't mind if the heat imposes silence, as long as the night is there to be enjoyed. From April to October, the locals become nocturnal.

In New York, on the other hand, true silence exerts itself. You step off a busy avenue into a dark restaurant as hushed and subdued as a library, every seat filled. Subway cars barrel and rattle through tunnels, the riders mute and blank-eyed, as though heading to their executions. And of course there is Wall Street after eight in the evening, when the cogs and wheels stop pumping out dollars. The huge yawning void seems like silence, even if it isn't. The background noise is the rumble of the infinite—silence listening to itself.

If someone has to scream to be heard, as often happens in Seville, I turn a deaf ear. It is in the act of living, not speaking, that Sevillians reveal their essence. New Yorkers don't want to live; they want to get things done. They speak directly, aware that time is scarce, assuming they will either be heard or intentionally ignored. If they see that they're wasting their breath, they abandon the conversation and think of another way to get their point across.

During a close and decisive match in Seville's professional soccer stadiums, a constant buzz of emotion reverberates from kickoff to the final whistle. There are ups and downs, moments when the clamor is not quite so clamorous, but the stadiums never lose their pitch of a public sounding off, as much to support the home team as to celebrate the very passion of its *afición* (fan base). In New York's stadiums and arenas, even during the most intensely fought championships, the ebb and flow of the action is more noticeable in the stands. Sometimes the murmur seems to disperse without a common cause; other times it takes on the latent power of a mantra mumbled by millions. New York fans always keep an eye on the game, but they save their energy and signature gestures for true euphoria and disappointment. As in every pursuit, New Yorkers seem to live for culminating moments, while Sevillians throw themselves without reserve into their passions and pleasures.

Seville at its best sounds like a packed bar with every last reveler at that early stage of drunkenness when they return momentarily, giddily, to youth. New York hitting on all cylinders evokes the cacophony of a mid-twentieth century newsroom filled with pounding typewriters, editors screaming into phones, and the thunder of the presses rolling downstairs. New York is like a classroom in which the teacher is capable of simultaneously stimulating and controlling the students. Seville is like a classroom where the students have the teacher in the palm of their capricious and occasionally cruel little hands. Both can be hotbeds of learning.

Seville is like a hive of bees overdosing on nectar. The activity is frenetic and florid, driven by a single aim: to extract from life the sweetest of all possible juices. The rules are rigid and the roles clear, having become instinct after thousands of years. An intruder, like me, is superfluous at best. If I am curious, attentive, and respectful, I'll be permitted to take part in the succulent harvest, although I shouldn't forget my protective suit.

New York is like a land overrun with lions accustomed to getting what they want where and when they want it. There are codes and laws, it's true, but the mightiest and most dangerous of the species are renegades that roam as their impulses and appetites dictate. All of us are their potential prey; they even eat their young. In the bush, intermittent roars alternate with the menacing hush of an endless, stalking pursuit. To ensure survival, you need to be dangerous, too.

LA VISTA

Seville is a walkway of monochromatic Mediterranean models.
The fairness of hair, skin, and eyes that a New Yorker might attribute
to a blonde hardly exists in Seville, except on tourists. *Una rubia
sevillana* (a Sevillian blonde) is more often than not a relatively light-
skinned brunette. When I first feasted my eyes on the sea of olive-
skinned beauty here, I felt as if birds of paradise were circling around
my head, twittering away, hailing my safe and triumphant arrival into
port. *So this is variety*, I said to myself, not yet realizing that I was
the variety.

For Seville's April Fair, tens of thousands of Sevillian
women squeeze into brightly patterned, torso-hugging, frilly-
bottomed flamenco dresses. Overwhelmed by so much color, I have
to resort to body type to tell the women apart. One will look as lean
and lithe as a cobra, another like a horn of womanly plenty welling
out from the waist up, another like a horn of womanly plenty welling
out from the waist down, another like a double-whammy of

womanly wellings-out, another like a slab of voluptuously carved and darkly varnished wood, as though born to beat down troubled seas with her broad, aerodynamic bosom. Without a hint of shame, these women exhibit their curves—firm, fallen, or overinflated. The grand majority carry it off with the cold-blooded brio of a slightly stuck-up bride.

New York is a walkway of top models. In Manhattan, where the world's beautiful people settle down in hopes of making it in the ruthless businesses of entertainment and fashion, the physical specimens on display have always seemed more like the apple of a fetishist's eye. To me, the real gems can be found in either the outer boroughs or the inner city, their beauty burning up their humble, working-class blocks. There are stunners who dress and make themselves up with the same sensual instinct as Sevillians, but their sexiness is secondary to expressing who they are. The women who know themselves triumph; those who dress against their natures fail spectacularly. A vanity fair of infinite variety: that's New York, both on the periphery and at the very heart of it.

Seville embodies light. After a sudden burst of rain in May, as the dust and heat rush gurgling through the gutters and down the drains, the streets and houses seem to shine. It is impossible to see with more clarity. At dusk, the light changes in tone until dark finally descends. Sepia and purple are the principal protagonists. They can reach the extremes of orange and violet without breaking harmony. I have seen psychedelic sunsets over the industrial zones of New Jersey in which the sky seems to scream with mental anguish. The Sevillian sun always sets with sobriety, giving off an almost repentant light, as though excusing itself for having beaten down for so many consecutive hours without respite.

New York embodies luminosity. My memories of my former city are so tied to artificial light that I struggle to imagine it in the plain light of day. For years I commuted to Manhattan on the Staten Island Ferry. On the way to work, I would sit on the eastern deck to watch the sun rise; on the trip home, I would sit on the western deck to watch it set. Before my attentive stare, the city lights would compete with the sun for prominence. At dawn, daybreak would begin to overtake the lights of its rival. At dusk, the city would increasingly stand out in the twilight. I would always be abandoning the stellar isle just as its star would begin to shine.

Seville is color. The happiest tones of the spectrum are reflected as much in the festivals as in the flowers of the blooming countryside. Blood red, jungle green, and pomegranate purple seem like scandalous stains beneath such a relentless and powerful sun, but, draped over pale marble, they give an added hint of coolness to a room darkened for the siesta or to the vestibule of a church receiving its faithful for midday Mass.

New York is reflection. Your image sticks to you more than your shadow. It follows you on the sly, waiting for the opportune moment to take you off guard in a panel of black glass. My father came home from work once and said, "Thanks to a storefront window, I now know for certain that I'm an old man."

Some reflections block out others. Three times a week for more than a quarter century, New York had reflected my father's image and name back at him from the pages of the New York *Daily News* and then *New York Newsday*, papers read by hundreds of thousands of people each day. On the other hand, when I came of age and tried to make my name in what my father called "the greatest city in the world," I felt like a faint dot of paint in some pointillist masterpiece, indistinguishable from the rest.

Seville is claustrophobia bordering on art. In the old town, the views are stunted and the streets narrow and serpentine. But once inside the labyrinth, the buildings loom high and the meandering lanes and tiny gated courtyards lure you in, promising surprises. They do not disappoint: a profusion of flowers explodes off a balcony; a cactus, its trunk as thick as a Spanish pine's, resembles a candelabra gone wild; three ancient temple columns, each a single piece of stone, rise two stories high; a disfigured Roman torso, as though buried up to the waist, is crammed into a sooty recess on a side street off the Alameda de Hércules.

New York is agoraphobia bordering on art. Its legendary verticality cannot really be grasped unless one has drifted like a speck at the bottom of it for years. One ends up developing a less deferential concept of height. In Seville, I live in a building known in the neighborhood as "*la torre*" (the tower). It is seven stories high. In New York, a seven-story building is called a walk-up because it doesn't have an elevator. Sevillians simply can't fathom this.

"What do pregnant women do? And the elderly?" they ask.

"Exercise," I reply.

New York's grand avenues, wide, straight, and flat enough to land a fleet of jet fighters, have always made the crowding and congestion bearable and almost buoyant for me, as though at any moment it could suddenly disperse. The suburbs reach southward to the outskirts of Philly and northward to the outskirts of Bean Town. The urban sprawl that spills out from US city centers reveals our innate arrogance and small-mindedness. Space is exploited without limit or shame. Boxy superstores squat along the sides of suburban drags. The parking lots that surround them seem impossible to fill, until the weekend arrives.

In Seville, the houses resemble rows of tiny, attached citadels. With grated windows and slab-like doors, they line up like European footballers defending on a set piece, shoulder to shoulder, hands protecting their privates, forming a barricade before the goal. Drying clothes flap like flags off roof terraces. Balconies are hardly ever used, except during Holy Week when the religious processions pass. Sometimes through an iron gate and a tunneled passageway, you'll spy a cool and spacious patio with lush potted plants, mahogany benches, and the sound of trickling water echoing off Mudéjar tiles. Such an inviting scene calls out like a honey trap.

In the more modern apartment blocks, windows are equipped with heavy-duty blinds called *persianas,* a kind of hard plastic version of those loot-proof store grates. Supposedly installed to block out the brutal summertime sun, the *persianas* are almost always drawn, no matter the time of day or year. In New York, a

French friend of mine used to shake his head at the iron fire escapes zigzagging down the façades of refurbished tenement houses.

"It is crossing out the architecture!" he would lament.

Persianas are a different kind of blight. Sevillian buildings teeming with life are made to look like Secret Service holding centers.

New York apartments resemble shop fronts. At first glance, the whole country seems immodest about exposing its inner sanctum to the outside world, as though our intention were to tantalize the passing public with our particular versions of domestic comfy-ness. In suburbia or in small towns, each house sits on its own parcel of land, often without fences to mark off the property. *Persianas* don't exist. As if laughing in the face of such a chaste idea, we fling wide the curtains of our living and dining rooms. Once the sun goes down, you can see directly into our illuminated hearths, as though even our privacy were up for sale.

The churches give pause, thank God. In Seville, they rise above the other architecture; in New York, the other architecture rises above them. The sight of Sevillian churches puts my head in the clouds, while the sight of New York churches puts my feet on the ground. Something similar occurs on cross-country car trips. The towns around Seville announce themselves to approaching travelers by the height of their bell towers. Everything else seems to spill down, like lava out of a volcano, cooled over centuries and covered in slaked lime. Travelers along US highways glimpse skylines surrounded by a haze of smog, an eyesore for sore eyes, although to my unaccustomed half orange they are miraculous apparitions.

EL OLFATO

Having settled down in Seville with wife and kids, I find myself living on the sixth floor of a seven-story apartment block. Our door is at the end of the right-hand prong of the U-shaped landing—precisely where odors accumulate and grow stale. At the very threshold of my home, not only can I smell what my neighbors are going to eat that day, I know what they ate a day or two before, especially when Anna and her deadbeat son leave their garbage bags outside the door to take downstairs later. When I step into the building's single elevator with barely the capacity for four adults, I can guess who the previous occupant was. Vestiges of dog, hangover, sweat, or cloying perfume give it away.

Actually, such packed-in living provokes more delight than disgust in me. I revel in the potpourri of foul and fragrant that wafts in and out of windows, up or down stairwells, and underneath doors. Perhaps the pleasure is the novelty. I was born and raised on Staten Island, where I can only recall the industrial perfume of fabric softener blowing out of dryer vents protruding from basement windows.

That's not exactly true. All of New York City's garbage was sent to Staten Island, to the Fresh Kills Landfill on the West Shore, for more than fifty years. When the dump finally closed in 2001, it had earned the notoriety of becoming the largest man-made object ever constructed, spanning over seven square miles. On my end of the island, the North Shore, we had to tolerate the fallout when the wind blew northeast. Imagine being stuck behind a city garbage truck doing pick-up rounds on a hot, muggy August afternoon.

The housing boom that took place around and on the very top of this fetid, decomposing pile of waste was my first great lesson in the extent to which people can kid themselves. The real estate moguls must have thought, "How can we possibly get rid of such obviously defective merchandise?" They could not have done it in grander style, selling it off to young couples from Brooklyn, often with or expecting children. Just to own something with a suburban sheen, these people left their tenement houses, which probably smelled like mine, for attached or semi-attached condos sunk in a smog of megapolitan rot.

During my first year in Seville, when I lived in the old town and would head off to work at the crack of dawn, the street cleaners would be out blasting the narrow, cobbled lanes with power hoses. Mist shot through with disinfectant would rise up around garbage bins and out of the nastier nooks and crannies of the lanes and alleys—a valiant attempt to combat the city's dog waste problem. I had arrived in the most storied city in Spain, hoping to be transported by the legendary orange blossom, only to have the sweet aroma overpowered by the chemical stench of poison.

What I miss most is the scent of the sea. To me, the ocean brings to mind fresh winds and an appetite for discovery. Seville is landlocked. While its cultural offerings are sophisticated and deep, they are also narrow—folkloric, with the city publishing stacks of well-documented but navel-gazing books about itself. Other options are generally second-rate, with the possible exception of opera. But

Málaga, just two hours away by train, has eclectic museums and ambitious plans. For lying on the hip Mediterranean coast, Málaga is a forward-thinking city open to change, while Seville remains a baroque altar piece with lots of fascinating little curlicues that curve inward and refer to itself.

The first time I visited Málaga, I went to dip my feet in the Mediterranean, expecting its mythic clarity. The water was as murky as New York Harbor. I was only in up to my knees but could no longer see my feet. I wondered, *If I lived in Málaga, would I get lost in the crowd, too?*

On its best days, Seville smells like the countryside in bloom. During my first summer in the city, I emerged one morning from my apartment, stunned to find the air awash in rosemary, as though a cloud of fragrance had enveloped the streets. Turned out the Corpus Christi procession had taken place that morning on a route strewn with herbs, now crushed into bits by the passing feet of the dispersed multitude. Mixed in with the effluvium of horse manure, it created a strangely intoxicating and thought-provoking blend.

Sevillian culture, like any culture worth its salt, cannot be separated into good and bad. It's a package deal: horseshit and aromatic spices. It's like the well-bred *estadounidense* who apologizes at the supermarket when it's the cashier's fault. The politeness is both heartfelt and pure hypocrisy. It's the stuff of art, art that you cannot find in museums.

It would make complete sense if fabric refreshers didn't exist in my adoptive city. Why would anyone choose them over the sun? I try to tell my half orange that there is nothing cleaner than fabrics washed with just water and unscented soap, then toasted rigid outdoors. But she will not be convinced. For special occasions, she'll even spray the wedges with *eau de toilette*.

On rainy days, the less hygienic citizens of both cities share the stink of sour milk, unmitigated by even the most eye-watering colognes. Sevillians wrongly call it *humedad* (humidity). Humidity is felt, not smelt. New Yorkers do not shy away from the rightful name: mildew. If assaulted by spores of it on the bus or metro, I get off as soon as possible. I don't care if I arrive late to class or my clothes get soaked in the rain. Anything to flush out the inside of my nose. I suspect New Yorkers put up with it because they have more important things to concern themselves with, or so they think, while Sevillians turn a plugged-up nose out of pride. To acknowledge its existence would be to admit that they are losing the battle against grime and germs in their very homes. The horror! The horror! Their homes are the only places, other than their churches, where cleanliness really matters to them.

I once read that Saint Camillus de Lellis' vocation to care for the sick was so intense that the fetor of bedpans and decomposing flesh sent him into raptures, while exquisite perfumes caused him to retch—in other words, why we like or dislike certain odors cannot be logically explained. Who knows what's behind my revulsion and delight? I can't stand mildew but am stimulated by the miasmas that accumulate before my front door. Both fabric refreshers and whiffs of municipal waste provoke sweet nostalgia in me. As far as mysteries go, *el olfato* seems surpassed only by...

EL TACTO

The pulse of New York grips me by the nape of the neck and walks beside me, blowing its hot, humid breath in my face and asking, "What are your plans? Are you using your time well?"

The pulse of Seville surprises me on the terrace of a sidewalk café, pounding me on the back, apparently glad to see me. If I accept the beer offered, I will have to hear a tirade filled with delusions of grandeur and torment about how life is *un martirio chino* (Chinese martyrdom).

To me, the feel of a place depends on the energy of its inhabitants. New Yorkers can be despotic—in how they bark out requirements when ordering a latte or stridently claim a patch of shade for themselves in Sheep Meadow in Central Park or get indignant when some inexperienced subway rider causes a holdup at a turnstile.

Back in the '90s, I went to a wedding at the Gramercy Park Hotel. As guests of the hotel, we had access to the park, which is an enclosed city block only open to those who live around it and pay a yearly fee. There were about twenty of us at the wedding, immaculately dressed and hushed by that cool, sylvan refuge. The pastor suggested that we step off the gravel path to stand under a towering pin oak to accompany the bride and groom as they exchanged vows. A spirit of intimacy and serendipity reigned, auguring well for long-lasting love. The pastor opened his prayer book and began the blessings when suddenly some Valkyrie of the neighborhood watch swooped down on us, shouting and gesturing frantically at the "Keep off the grass" sign obscured in a bed of pachysandra at our feet.

That self-appointed guardian of Gramercy Park, warding off evil turf traipsers, happens to have a Sevillian counterpart. I came across him one evening in *la Capilla de los Marineros* (the Seamen's Chapel) after Mass, ripping into the churchgoing public for talking too loudly in the presence of *Nuestra Señora de la Esperanza* (Our Lady of Hope), a statue. I suspect that the Virgin, if her spirit happened to be near, felt more ashamed of that haughty and disdainful reproach in her name than of the noisy chatter. But the scolded faithful knew how to respond, lowering their voices for a few seconds, then letting them rise again, even louder than before.

In Seville, as in New York, horns honk insistently from the back of a line of traffic because a driver at the front has a tricky maneuver to make. That time at the Alcampo customer service counter, when I was slow doing the math and got an earful for it, is by no means anomalous. Once, my half orange, filling up our car tires at a Sevillian service station, took longer than she might have because four-year-old Wedge One wanted to work the air hose. The lady next in line lowered her driver's side window and said, "*No tenemos todo el día.*" (We don't have all day.)

"*Se contagia tu alegría, hija mía,*" (Your joy is contagious, daughter of mine,) said my wife, making sure Wedge One took his own sweet time. Then she returned home furious.

"And you say you'd like to live in New York!" I said.

Back in 1914, the Sevillian poet José María Izquierdo dubbed his hometown "*la Ciudad de la Gracia*" (the City of Panache), which remains accurate in my opinion. Everything Sevillians love—watching soccer, bantering at the bar or at the butcher's, taking to the public thoroughfare, staging their religious and folkloric festivals—they do with palpable flair. Could it be that the flipside of that panache is a combination of impatience and permissiveness? For example, Sevillians put all their panache into complaining passionately about their superiors and subordinates at work, their neighbors, their doctors, their children's teachers, their children, and, of course, politicians, for living *de puta madre* (like mother whores). Yet when it comes time to act, Sevillians throw up their hands, leaving all problems that do not directly strip them of home and livelihood in the hands of the same political office seekers they rail against. In other words, protesting does not mean getting down to business; it means blowing off steam in tremendous shows of bravado. *Ser listo* (to be clever) does not mean knowing how to take action but knowing how not to take it, except when protecting and preserving the complacency and comfort of one's tiny, tightly-knit clan.

The more time I spend in Seville, the more I feel like hurling myself against the citizens to knock some community resolve into them.

For thirty-six years, I lived as a peace-loving man, apparently immune to New York's volatility; then I moved to Seville and the beast emerged. Once, on my way to the April Fair, I punched the hood of a BMW M3 because its driver had illegally parked on the sidewalk and was now leaning on his horn to harass the mob that impeded him from pulling out of his prohibited space. I needed him to know that his flouting of the rules and unabashed boorishness could lead to ugly consequences.

Another time, in front of a popular night spot on a crowded street in the city center I saw a young punk in a motorcycle helmet head-butt his girlfriend so hard that she staggered back and her knees buckled. After finding her legs, she approached him again, indulgent, imploring. It took every ounce of my restraint not to take him down with a running tackle, knowing that this lovesick girl would probably feel the pain as much or more than he did. I yearned to punish them both.

Perhaps these new violent impulses come from having switched from a language I had mastered to another that I regularly mangle, especially when worked up. The sharp and clever tongue that once got me out of jams has become dull and defective; it's often at a loss for words. Stripped of my weapon of choice, perhaps I've become jumpy and cantankerous. Or maybe *I'm* the one pawing at the ground with no real intention of charging. Maybe the ever-present threat of backlash kept me in check in New York, while I beat my chest in Seville because I feel like no one will challenge me.

Three generations ago, just before the Spanish Civil War, Seville was known and feared for its political passions and convictions. So what happened? Did the nationalist rebels' bloody repression, the wanton tossing of grenades into humble working class homes, regardless of the women and children huddling within, and the thousands of public executions without trial that occurred in the days and months after Lieutenant General Queipo de Llano captured the city annihilate Sevillians' fighting spirit once and for all, at least as far as public causes are concerned? Or—the most chilling possibility of all—were Sevillians just beaten at their own game? Punishing and killing without pity, care, or control smacks to a terrifying degree of those twisted twin sisters of panache: impatience and permissiveness.

New York and Seville are overcharged cities: Seville full of sound and fury apparently signifying nothing, and New York fully loaded and trigger-happy. That's what I say now. But if a sudden wave of brutality washes over my adoptive city and no one takes the trouble to stand their ground and resist it, not even the jumpy and cantankerous New Yorker, I'll want to define the cities the other way around.

EL GUSTO

To me, New York is pizza, calzones, hot dogs, bagels, knishes, and moussaka—all foods introduced by immigrants and then given a local twist. There is also diner food, which I recommend to Sevillians visiting New York as the only kind of quick, cheap, all-American meal they can grab that will have any real personality. Of course, New York serves spectacular ethnic food in its purest form, too—dim sum in Chinatown, *arroz a la cubana* and fried plantains in Washington Heights, Moroccan meat pies in Astoria, Queens. I could go on. Sevillians like to snicker at what New Yorkers drink—stainless steel thermoses constantly at our lips, filled with watered-down coffee, or one can after another of Coca-Cola Zero. Sure, we have our vulgar habits to get us through our dog-eat-dog days, but let's not forget that only in my hometown can you get a perfectly chilled dry martini, a bloody Mary as savory as the best gazpacho, or tropical fruit juice with your franks at Papaya King.

If you've been spoiled by New York, then I wouldn't recommend the ethnic food in Seville (with the possible exception of Moroccan, since the traditions come from just across the Strait of Gibraltar). By ethnic food, I also mean hamburgers and hot dogs. Sevillians don't understand US fast food. They think it's easy; they have no idea about toppings and sauces. In Seville, stick to the local dishes: gazpacho in summer, just a smidgen below freezing—like the beer!—and absolutely nothing like the chunks of vegetables floating in cold, oily water that I've seen pawned off as the authentic article in the States. In winter, *cuchareo* (spoon food)—basically stews made with lentils, beans, or chickpeas and flavored with pork fat and sausage—will warm you up, stimulate your taste buds, and stick to your ribs. Year-round, I recommend the meat, Iberian of course. Sevillians cook it just right, serving it sprinkled with salt and sometimes crisped sprigs of rosemary, nothing else. Spaniards get a bad rap for using too much salt and garlic. It definitely happens, often to hide poorly prepared food, but next time just go to a better restaurant.

Tapa, supposedly an international word, is generally misused in the States. The common term "Spanish *tapas* restaurant" is not only redundant (*tapa* is by definition Spanish) and grammatically bizarre (imagine saying "an Italian pastas and pizzas restaurant"), it is a contradiction in terms: one does not eat *tapas* in a restaurant but in a bar. A *tapa* is a small dish of food to pick at while drinking your beer or wine, to make it more tasty and satisfying. In Seville, when the locals go for *tapas*, they don't sit down at a table and order lots of little dishes of food, like a smorgasbord of hors d'oeuvres; they bar-hop, snacking at one or two small dishes or *montaditos* (mini-sandwiches) in each place before moving on to the next. Some bars are known for a particular specialty, perhaps *rabo de toro* (stewed bull's tail) or *caracoles* (snails) when in season, or *montaditos de pringá* (fried bacon fat sandwiches), or *migas* (breadcrumbs fried with sausage and garlic, often accompanied by a slice of orange, that call to my mind Thanksgiving stuffing).

Eating a *tapas* feast can take hours, with the after-dinner constitutional converted into many mid-course ones. In its original version, *tapear* (to go for *tapas*) means to go on a gastronomically-centered pub crawl.

As far as local delicacies, I would be remiss if I didn't mention *jamón* (Iberian cured ham). Tourists visiting Andalusia for the first time are often struck by the rows of cured pig legs hanging from the ceilings of bars and cafés, with little cardboard elbows or plastic cups attached to the bottoms to absorb or catch the dripping grease. We *estadounidenses* just aren't used to such public exhibition—in restaurants!—of the dismembered limbs of animals soon to be served up as meals.

The best Iberian ham comes from black pigs raised wild on huge tracts of land and fed only Spanish acorns, oblong and mouth-watering nuts that lack the bitter resin of those that fall from North American oaks. Pigs fattened on such fare produce a naturally sweet meat, which is then enhanced by the salt of curation.

When served at room temperature, little beads of clean, nutty oil form on the ham's surface. Putting just a finger-sized sliver on my tongue, I find that my saliva suddenly becomes the most delicious and satisfying elixir on earth. Every last one of my taste buds becomes fully engaged in the savoring. Best of all, unlike other great tastes that have marked me—New York pizza, my mother's blueberry pie, Spanish potatoes and eggs—*jamón* doesn't provoke in me a compulsive desire to overeat. I only want to delight in the *exquisitez* of the moment.

But taste has to do with more than just the tongue. To me, it also takes in style, manners, and preferences; it's all five senses working together to receive and sort through stimuli, helping us to discern what is both unique and universal about ourselves.

Taste is the king of the senses; the others exist just to serve it.

Which isn't to say that nobility had anything to do with forming my taste. I began deliberately cultivating it the moment I began trying to impress and attract girls, who, unlike my other friends, seemed to appreciate music for more than pulsing rhythms, stories for more than action, dance for more than physical release, nature for more than its grandeur, and alcohol for more than its capacity to inebriate. Turned out that the so-called "infinite ways to a woman's heart" all came down to either the doggedness of my pursuit or to the coolness with which I hid my panting interest— that is, to either going all out or playing hard to get. Staying power has always been my forte, never coolness. And so, settling in for the long haul, I set out to beat women at their own game, and in that way magnified how I saw the world.

As one would expect, when I fell in love, refinement became revolution. Life turned into a feast for the senses. So just imagine when I fell in love with The One! My half orange was the biggest revolution of all.

A couple of months in, with our initial passion yet to abate, I decided it was time to put her to the test.

"Would you like to have children one day?" I asked.

It was a standard question in my repertoire. I expected a deflection, not a response, something contrived to not frighten me away. This would have permitted us to carry on as we had been, having a ball for a few more weeks or perhaps even months, however long the favorable winds lasted, with her spurred on by the false hope of getting me to commit, and with me relieved to have my conscience clear.

"Of course I want children," she replied, "but first I have to fall in love with a man worthy of fathering them."

Her absolute lack of bullshit blew me away.

"That's me!" I felt the urge to say.

From then on, she became a kind of living manual that I could consult on *saber estar* (knowing how to be), which we might as well just call *gusto* (taste)—how we manage to either defy clichés or shed light on them.

We moved in together in April. April in Seville! Finally I was able to float on the bouquet of orange blossoms, uncut by the city's sanitary measures. At the April Fair, I was a guest to the humming hive, sipping on nectar at my pleasure, thanks to my very own voluptuously carved, olive-skinned beauty, exquisitely wrapped in frilly, polka-dotted finery.

When the women got up to dance, one of her friends' boyfriends turned to me and asked, "You like Spanish women?"

I looked out at the dance floor and stared.

"I like *her*," I said.

Thanks to my half orange, my palate began to assimilate all the flavors of the feast.

TALES OF TWO CITIES

ON THE FRINGE

Calling myself a New Yorker gives a false impression. Actually I'm a Staten Islander, from New York's "forgotten borough," where you find no skyscrapers, grand avenues, or celebrities; no cutting edge, no cultured multitude, no thrilling and unceasing roar. Although New York is called "The City That Never Sleeps," Staten Island sleeps, sometimes even during the day.

The closest thing to a tourist attraction on Staten Island is the ferry that takes its residents to Manhattan, but, more to the point, brings them back. It's free, a nice perk to the fifty-or-so thousand Staten Islanders who commute to work every day. But for the tourists who take it in order to see the New York skyline from its stunning southern vantage point or the Statue of Liberty from the calm center of the harbor, this non-existent price implies that they are travelling to a no-place. Upon disembarking in the Staten Island Ferry terminal, they follow signs back to the entrance hall and simply wait for the next ferry back to Manhattan.

Other than the ferry, the borough used to be known for the previously mentioned dump. When it finally closed, some city planners suggested in all seriousness that the mountains of buried rubbish be converted into a ski resort.

Only once in my thirty-six years as a Staten Island resident did I believe that being considered the bumpkins on the stinking hill would work to our benefit—when the Twin Towers fell. Lots of Staten Islanders, myself included, lined up along the northern shore, looking across the harbor with a mixture of longing, rage, and fear at what only hours before had been perhaps New York's most emblematic buildings. But we longed, raged, and feared from afar, assuming that the terrorists would pass over a backwater like ours. Turns out that we did not escape unharmed. Many of the 274 Staten Islanders who died that day were the firemen, cops, and medical technicians who went charging, hellbent, to do what they perhaps knew would be the last thing they ever did.

I love my hometown—because it's my hometown and because I grew up happy there—but when Sevillians ask me where I'm from, I tell them New York City. People either love or hate it, but either way, my association with the place gives me instant cachet.

Saying I live in Seville will impress *estadounidenses* almost as much. Those who have not visited the city no doubt imagine me in a quaint and picturesque European setting that plays on all the old Spanish clichés; and those who have visited it probably imagine, well, more or less the same thing, since during their brief stay, they never set foot out of the old city.

My half orange's apartment is in Madre de Dios (Mother of God), on the outskirts of the city. After moving in with her, when well-off Sevillians would ask where I lived, I'd make a point to say, "Madre de Dios—the neighborhood, not the street." The street is one of the narrow, curving, cobbled lanes of Santa Cruz, the high-rent district, while the neighborhood runs from the edge to the heart of one of the city's more notorious low-rent districts, Tres Barrios (Three Neighborhoods), the names of which I love: Madre de Dios, Candelaria (Candlemas) and Pajaritos (Little Birds).

In most US cities, the downtowns empty out when the workday ends. In Andalusia, people live in the city centers, with the periphery reserved for those of more modest means. While in English the word "suburb" evokes tree-lined streets, expansive lawns, and two-car garages attached to palatial homes, the Spanish word *suburbio* evokes bleak, industrial wastelands and teeming, beat-to-hell housing projects. What both worlds have in common is a clear border between the urban and the suburban.

Back in the late '80s, when I went to college in Davidson, North Carolina, the phrase "to live on the other side of the railroad tracks" still applied. The poor—and, of course, blacks—lived on the side of the railroad tracks that the college wasn't on. On Staten Island, the demarcation line was the Staten Island Expressway. On

the northern side of it, you could find Borough Hall and the court buildings but also the island's ten housing projects, which caused the primarily white, middle-class population to begin moving to the South Shore or New Jersey. Worries about safety, the quality of the schools, and decreasing real estate values were exacerbated by racial issues.

I grew up in Westerleigh, officially on the "wrong" side of the Staten Island Expressway, but seamlessly white and working-class. Each family was neatly installed on its quarter-acre plot of land, with leafy backyards and garage-mounted basketball hoops. While I clearly grew up more suburban than urban, people at Davidson held me up as a product of the mean streets, which was fine by me. I had the option to choose city or suburban kid as I saw fit.

Being a resident *guiri* in Seville is not much different. Strictly speaking, I can call myself an immigrant, but with none of the struggles that the word implies. As an *estadounidense* of a certain class and race, I always had the option of going home to the land of opportunities if things got too rough. Like many of my tribe, I tend to overcompensate for feeling like I've had it too easy. I take guilty pleasure in living with my half orange and wedges in an apartment building just on the "wrong" side of the Tamarguillo Beltway. Only one hundred meters on the other side, heading towards the city center, real estate prices double, sometimes triple, and the schools enjoy a good name. On the other hand, a block behind our building, unemployment rises to a whopping 75 percent. Madre de Dios is by no means a slum, but I like that living here means that neither the white- nor the blue-collar Sevillians can tag me right off.

A *guiri* living in Tres Barrios? Is he a hippie squatter? Did he get married to a stunner of a Spanish gypsy? Is he one of those wacky foreigners who wants to learn flamenco like a militant and renegade anthropologist, living among the tribes that carry it in their blood? To be honest, I have no idea what people think, because when I tell them where I live, they normally either shut up or change the subject. Once again, thanks to my privileges of birth, I can live in happy limbo, challenging people's assumptions.

The pull-no-punches Sevillian journalist Antonio Guerra once said, "Whoever wants to expose the hidden side of this city will experience the misfortune of being told, 'You are not one of us.'" When my Sevillian neighbors, dressed to the nines, announce that they're heading downtown, it reminds me of the old days: my friends and I on a Friday night, riding the Staten Island Ferry into Manhattan, thinking, *We're going to the city!*—as if we didn't already live there, as if Lady Liberty's illumination to a sophisticated new world would extinguish as soon as we returned home.

I moved from the forgotten part of one great city to the forgotten part of another. I soon discovered other similarities—for instance, that my neighbors generally preferred to be among their own except when taking day-trips to where they thought the real action was.

THE FOREIGNER'S NEIGHBORS

The foreigner, recently moved into his girlfriend's apartment, felt fortunate to be able to look down at the park in front, although it seemed more like an abandoned lot up close. The enormous sign announcing that it was under construction, or was about to be, gave him hope—false hope, it turned out. Five years passed, the foreigner was now married with children, and the park remained a wreck. Even the sign had been destroyed.

Children never went to the park to play, or young lovers to stroll, or families to have picnics. Only dogs entered to befoul it, with their owners looking the other way. At night, juveniles (both young and not so young) skulked around the borders, enjoying not the park itself but the stupefying substances they brought there. They only came to break things already broken or to do the same as the dogs did during the day. And they always left their garbage along the edges—empty booze bottles, drug paraphernalia, fast-food packaging, condoms, and their babies' dirty diapers. Because the park had been plagued by hard luck for so long without anyone trying to remedy it, the foreigner wondered if perhaps the neighborhood and the city government preferred a filthy and abandoned park, so that they could continue mistreating it while blaming each other for its disgraceful state.

But the neighborhood was changing. *Americanos* (not from the United States) had begun to move in. These people missed the wild and open country they had been born and raised in. Very few owned cars, and those who did had no friends or family in nearby villages to welcome them for *ferias*, *carnavales*, and *romerías*. Very often, entire clans shared the same living space, with low ceilings and paltry natural light. Barred windows looked out toward other barred windows, across stinking and stained courtyards, where the spare parts and stripped frames of motor scooters were chained to sickly and stunted trees. Living like this allowed them to make ends meet and send the little bit extra to the loved ones they had left back in their homelands. These people did not ask for much, did not ask for much of anything at all; they were even willing to settle for blight pawned off as a park.

One day, the foreigner's next-door neighbors, even newer to the building, neighborhood, and country than he, installed themselves around the park's sturdiest tree, and guests started showing up. Most of the trees had dried up, rotted, and come crashing down. Only the tree picked by the foreigner's neighbors provided the assurance and shade necessary to receive such a gathering of aunts, uncles, cousins, and of course friends, with their gaggles of children, and beach chairs and fold-out tables and Styrofoam crates filled with fare to feed the multitude. They set up a makeshift grill in a corner created by two crumbling cinderblock walls where bonfires had been lit by deadbeats during the winter. The foreigner's neighbors spent the whole afternoon there, mounting their very own *romería*, packing up only after night fell. They took their garbage with them. Having witnessed the ambiance, the foreigner suddenly resented his mortgage payments a bit less.

The next weekend more of the foreigner's neighbors' clan showed up, and the following weekend still more. Soon, on Saturdays and Sundays, from noon till nightfall, they overran the place. One way or another, they found space and shade to put their tables and chairs, to grill and season their meats, to make their music, and to celebrate birthdays amidst the jubilant cries of their young. Since the park's courts and playing fields had fallen into disrepair, these people brought their own equipment and took it away after playing their games. They always left the park in the same state they had found it in.

More than once, the foreigner's neighbors, upon seeing him return from his errands with a look of approval on his face, invited him to drop off his bags upstairs and come back down with his tiny clan. The foreigner planned to accept the invitation one day. He looked forward to taking part in the revolution that had transformed the great eyesore of his neighborhood into a family fairgrounds and a recurring feast.

But like all revolutions, this one met resistance. To the more established neighbors, the sudden state of grace of their park was cause for alarm, not joy. The "*peste de barbacoa*" (stink of barbecue) clung to the laundry they hung out in the afternoons, they complained. They apparently preferred their clothes to absorb the odor of backed-up sewers and fecal dust. These self-proclaimed "*vecinos de toda la vida*" (lifelong residents) who spent all afternoon indoors with the windows shut and their televisions on, blocking out the world pissed and shit on by their dogs and delinquent children, began denouncing this advent of open-air diversion as "*una amenaza pública*" (a public threat). All of a sudden, the naysayers began to notice the litter strewn along the edges of the park, the ashes of the bonfires from the winter before, and the broken and charred remains of the discarded furniture that had fed them, and they blamed the recent arrivals for destroying the neighborhood's—get this!— "*paseo arbolado*" (wooded promenade).

One weekend afternoon, as the park brimmed with barbecues and volleyball and birthday parties and impromptu music, someone called the cops and they came—almost unheard of in Madre de Dios when it came to nuisance complaints. Not only that, they came in force, with paddy wagons, helmets, and riot gear, spoiling the party once and for all. The foreigner's neighbors' clan quietly packed up and left, in search of peace, not problems—proof that they had been deliberately misunderstood.

The park went back to being abandoned, and the long-standing neighbors puffed up with pride, like children who had managed to get borrowed toys back only to break them on purpose before the eyes of their imagined rivals. It was the only time the foreigner had ever seen his adoptive neighborhood and city work together efficiently—to expel people who knew how to make the most of what the locals had long ago forgotten to value or appreciate.

"What can we do," the foreigner's neighbors said to him, "if their dogs come first?"

OPEN DOORS

Back in my twenties and early thirties, I lived in a building with seventeen floors and more than two hundred apartments. Other than the doormen, I never managed to get to know anyone, except for a woman from Mexico City who made eye contact and struck up conversations in elevators, a habit that disconcerted the rest of us. Sometimes she would actually hold open the elevator doors to finish what she was saying.

My New York neighbors had been disembodied persons to me. The guy next door had various lovers, which I knew because of the different ways they let rip in the moment of moments. But I never laid eyes on any of them, nor on the lover boy himself. I suspected that, like me, he never left his apartment if he heard neighbors on the landing.

My next door neighbor on the other side kept to herself, too. Once I rang her bell to say that her cat was using my balcony as a litter box. I had to make my complaint through the peep hole because she would not open the door. She apologized profusely through the two inches of solid oak that separated us, saying that it would never happen again. And it didn't.

"Good fences make good neighbors," says the wall-mender in Robert Frost's famous poem.

They had certainly made it easier for my New York neighbors and me to take each other's quirks and unintended slights less personally.

Then I moved to Seville, and a year later settled into my half orange's building, where doors tend to remain wide open. At first, the residents eyed me with suspicion, which only grew, as my half orange did, bigger and bigger with Wedge One. Like my mother-in-law, they probably worried I would bolt back to the States, either with or without the wedge. I ended up surprising them all, staying

home with him and carrying him around on neighborhood errands while my half orange was at work. Soon Wedge One was joined by Wedge Two, basically Irish twins, and I stayed home with them both. We became a common sight in and around the building. In the early afternoon when my half orange got home, I would pass her the baton and head off "to the job I get paid for," as I put it to my neighbors, who now talked to me not only in the elevator, but from balcony to balcony when we hung out clothes to dry, and even from landing to landing, through an echoing stairwell, when they heard the wedges wail.

"Which one had trouble sleeping last night, poor guy?" Rafa, the resident super, once shouted up from the floor below, acknowledging the thinness of the walls with all the naturalness in the world. Had that comment come from a New York neighbor, I would have thought he was insinuating that I should soundproof my fuckin' apartment, for Chrissake.

If one of the wedges threw a tantrum on the way in or out of our apartment, Ana, Isabel, Pepi, and/or Concha, all of them grandmothers, would stick their heads out their doors with sucking candies in hand, hoping to give consolation. Sometimes on the weekend, I would be out in the street on my own and would run into a resident a few blocks away. He or she would tell me exactly where I could find my wife and kids, having just seen them pass in such and such direction, along such and such street, most likely going to such and such playground. I would try to be gracious, thanking them for the information, and then would continue on my way. My neighbor would call out to me again, now pointing with near hysterical gesticulations toward where my half orange and wedges had supposedly been heading. I would smile insipidly and nod, then wave and turn away again, while my neighbor stood there stunned, no doubt wondering how long it would take me to finally learn the language.

Open doors, by the way, do make responsible neighbors, if not always good ones. Like the day when, for the third time in as many months, dirty water began to fall through our bathroom ceiling. The upstairs neighbor, a city street sweeper—in other words, a man who earned more than my wife and I combined, and who didn't have a mortgage to pay—had the gall to cry poverty when I'd gone upstairs and asked him to fix his faulty plumbing. This time, the water did not just seep through the ceiling but came down in buckets. I left my wedges in the playpen with my door wide open, so my neighbors could look in and shake their heads at the mayhem. Then I stomped upstairs and pounded on the shirker's door. To my surprise, he opened up. I managed to shame him into coming down to witness the scene. He saw the unrelenting cascade of dirty water, the bathroom and hallway flooding, and my sons looking confused and scared at the hullabaloo and at their dad's impotent red-faced fury. Even more importantly, he saw that all the neighbors were seeing it, the same neighbors who were aware that he was months behind on his community maintenance fees despite bringing in triple what they did with their measly pensions. And then, with perfect timing, my half orange returned from work and let the now more or less pilloried street sweeper have it as only an enraged Sevillian mother can. So all the neighbors, with their doors wide open, got the backstory with the i's dotted and the t's crossed, as well as a first-rate flamenco recital. Finally the resident *guiri* stepped in with the crowning blow, shouting in his slow, *seviyorkino*-accented Spanish, fraught with stuttering incredulousness, "*¡El tío ni siquiera tiene seguro de hogar!*" (The guy doesn't even have homeowner's insurance!)

In the end, open doors, three or more floors of them, made my neighbor forget his poverty. Ten days later he had new plumbing and we had a new ceiling.

Living all bunched up in the same building has its downside, of course. Once, so she wouldn't have to hear any more of a howling argument between Ana and her son, my wife put on the acclaimed *cantaor* (flamenco singer) Manuel de Angustias at full volume singing "Canalla" (Swine). Perhaps it was just coincidence, but when the song finished with the refrain "*¡Canalla! ¡Canalla! ¡Hablar por* *hablar!*' (Swine! Swine! You talk for the sake of talking!), the spat had ceased.

Then there are the smelly stairwells and landings. Rafa actually *smokes* in the building's single elevator. The super, for God's sake! The same guy who put up the "No smoking" stickers! His only concession is not to take drags when the doors are closed, but he keeps the butt lit even if he's packed in there with me and the wedges. Isabel from across the hall has the habit of leaving her fish-stinking garbage outside her door, sometimes for almost twenty-four hours, before taking it downstairs.

"So my cats don't go crazy," she explains. (Apparently not only dogs come before people in Madre de Dios.)

But all this is somehow bearable because I know my neighbors, not because I don't.

SURPRISED BY JOY

The first time I tried *jamón*, it was limp and clammy like raw bacon and made me want to gag. But just after Wedge One was born, a friend of my wife's brought over a plate of *jamón* cut into flake-like slices that disintegrated into eruptions of salty sweetness on my tongue. One experience seemed to have nothing to do with the other.

In my efforts to understand bullfighting, I have seen novices so blundering that they might as well have been country delinquents in harlequin suits, spearing stray animals in the public square. But twice, purely by chance, I saw a scrawny teenager named Emilio Delgado from Écija, whose poise with the cape and the sword convinced me without a shadow of a doubt that I would never be the man and artist he was, and that the four feisty bulls that he tangled with died in glory.

In the world of flamenco, there are hoofers and crooners with bodies and voices as poorly cared for as their repertoires. The so-called "pure" school of flamenco to which they claim to belong seems only a lame excuse for them to be artistically lazy and to perform the same schtick over and over, with pinched faces of feigned suffering. But once, at Seville's Teatro Central, I saw the *bailaor* (flamenco dancer) Israel Galván perform *Arena*. With daggers attached to his shoes and a poker face, he danced a duet with a rocking chair, his symbol for the Iberian bull, or perhaps for what he believed the Spanish had reduced it to. I instantly became a fan.

When it comes to *jamón*, bullfighting, and flamenco—a heavy-hitting Spanish cultural triumvirate if there ever was one— neither bad nor good applies. Only gross or sublime, vile or exquisite. It's impossible to remain on the fence. You're either for or against, a lover or a hater, although sometimes it depends on the day or even the moment. Earthly limbo, as many Sevillians will be the first to tell you, only exists in other cities.

Seville's three main *fiestas*—*Semana Santa* (Holy Week), *la Feria de Abril* (the April Fair), and the pilgrimage to El Rocío—seem organized to officially celebrate this idea. Each one drags on for a week, pushing overkill. All the better to blow us away unexpectedly.

The celebration of *Semana Santa* is Catholic religious faith taken to the extreme of spectacle. From Palm Sunday to early Easter Sunday morning, the entire city converts into an open-air museum with works of chillingly life-like baroque religious sculpture, some pieces over four hundred years old, weighing two to four tons, being carried through the teeming streets on the shoulders of religious strongmen who step out in perfect unison to Spanish marches or dirges. The processions in front of and behind the floats can have more than three thousand penitents donning the brotherhood's signature hoods and robes. Each procession starts at a parish church and takes a specific route to the Seville Cathedral, where respects are paid in front of the main altar, before returning sometimes over twelve hours later.

If you live in the city center, this is a colossal nuisance. The procession will wall you in if you cross the street for a carton of milk at an inopportune moment.

The first time I ever saw a religious float pass by up close, a procession was blocking me from my front door, twenty-five yards away. I settled in, bracing myself for boredom, until the float emerged from between two buildings, accompanied only by the sound of its bearers' traipsing feet. Just like that, I was brought back to a safari I once took in Tanzania, when an elephant whisked by our parked Range Rover, not lumbering and shaking the earth as I expected it to, but moving as if levitating.

For the next forty-five minutes, as the city's *fiesta* detained me, I thought about the ardent crusade of volunteers who were not only willing but yearned to send their priceless and irreplaceable works of art out into the streets, putting them at the mercy of the

tumultuous mob, of the fickle spring skies, or of any hater or fanatic who might be lying in wait, to make the Holy Spirit palpable to us.

It was as though the city were saying, Here are our most beloved and prized possessions, both spiritually and materially. We entrust them to you, whoever you are, Sevillian or not, believer or not, to love with all your heart and soul, or not. As you wish.

My first Easter Sunday in Seville, I went out into the street at noon, curious to see the grand finale. I expected to be floored. But when I made it down to the Cathedral, it was shut up tight except for the tourist entrance. The wooden chairs that had been set up all week in rows along the final stretch were being stacked and loaded into trucks. The party was over! Then it hit me. The *fiesta* had finished in the exact moment that, according to the Gospels, Christ's pain and suffering had lifted, as if the whole flamboyant spectacle had been to prevent His ordeal from oppressing the city.

A couple of weeks after *Semana Santa*, Sevillians outdo themselves again, this time with *la Feria de Abril*. Basically they move to the other side of the river into a makeshift tent city, strung with carnival lights and stinking of horse manure, to dress from another century and eat, drink, and dance the days and nights away. *El alumbrao*, or the official lighting at midnight of the *portada* (main gate) gets Sevillians in the holiday spirit just like the lighting of the tree in Rockefeller Center gets New Yorkers primed for Christmas.

Passing through the *portada* at night is like rising up from the New York City Subway and being assaulted by the blinking, neon-plated canyon walls of Times Square. The first impression of the lights, noise, colors, and shifting throng is impossible to forget. Then it gets old, sort of, until it pulls you back in. One night, returning from the *Feria* at 4 a.m., exhausted and already ready to call it a week, I passed one of the canvas tents with the sides wide open and music blaring and witnessed over fifty women, dressed in *trajes de gitana* (gypsy dresses), spin and dip and rotate their arms and wrists above their heads, all in perfect unison—a spontaneous happening that looked as if it had been rehearsed for centuries.

The next night I was back, enduring the crowds and the heat again, eager for more.

After *Feria*, the merrymaking continues with the pilgrimage to El Rocío, a village about an hour by car from Seville, although the hardcore *rocieros* go by covered wagon. The event can draw more than a million pilgrims during Pentecost weekend to venerate the statue of the Virgin, Blanca Paloma (White Dove), housed in an enormous, immaculately white "hermitage" that will appear to the average tourist like a cathedral by the sea.

After the rosary is recited at midnight on Sunday in the now-packed hermitage, the clichéd Spanish character is unleashed in unparalleled fashion, thanks to *el salto de la reja* (the jumping of the high iron fence that surrounds Blanca Paloma). In what looks to the unaccustomed eye like a spontaneous insurrection of the masses, young men begin to launch themselves over the fence and each other, fighting for the privilege to carry the Virgin out of the sanctuary into the mob of waiting faithful that spills into the teeming, dust-clouded streets (unpaved in El Rocío, like some town from the Wild West). Once Blanca Paloma emerges into open air, she is capable of causing what can only be described as irresponsible acts of religious fervor. In one famous case, caught on video, a screaming toddler was passed over the top of the crowd to kiss the Virgin's base.

Among the many miracles that Blanca Paloma is said to have performed, the most indisputable in my opinion is that nobody has ever gotten trampled to death after midnight on Pentecostal Sunday.

The illustrious Sevillian historian Antonio Domínguez Ortiz once wrote about "the immense contrasts" of the Seville in which he grew up: "the poetry and the filth, the opulence and the misery, the hovels beside the grandiose monuments." He might also have added the mundane and the miraculous.

Quality control, a US specialty, is certainly essential in matters of life and death, but it backfires when the goal is transcendence. If the main objective is to avoid dissatisfaction, then probably satisfaction is the best you're going to get. Seville's top-shelf cultural offerings will disgust, bore, or dissatisfy me four out of five times, then suddenly give me a taste or glimpse of heaven.

One evening at a neighborhood café, I ordered a *serranito* (little highlander sandwich). The hero roll was fresh and lightly toasted, crispy on the outside and steamy-soft on the inside; the sautéed chicken breast had been cooked just right, charred slightly to seal in the juice; the *jamón* was tender, secreting its nutty oil; and the green pepper was plump and hot, providing succulent splashes of tangy flavor. Simply out of this world.

But when I returned a few days later for another one, the bread was stale, the chicken tough, the *jamón* leathery, and the pepper mushy and cold. I did not send the hellish *serranito* back, just picked at it, because I knew that soon enough I would be eating another heavenly one, and would enjoy it more for not having taken it for granted.

MOTHER OF GOD'S TWO-BIT SAINT

Every morning, the wedges and I walked a few blocks to buy fruit, vegetables, and freshly baked bread at La Tiendesita (The Little Shop, purposely misspelled with an "s" instead of a "c" to celebrate *andalú*). There were some benches in the plaza out front where a certain neighborhood element congregated at almost all hours to drink forties and get high.

They were a cheerful crew—at least when in an altered state—always pleased to see the *guiri* arrive with his two mini-*guiris*. We often stopped to chat. Sometimes a young woman would be with them, perhaps twenty-five years old. She would have been pretty if not for the hangdog, strung-out look of an addict. Word was that her mother had been awarded full custody of her two children and wouldn't let her see them. Then the youngest had died of a rare disease. Now she was clearly pregnant again.

When she saw my boys, she would take them on her lap and hug and kiss them. Sometimes she would unbutton their pants to tuck their shirts in. All this with cigarette in hand, while exhaling smoke from the side of her mouth.

La Tiendesita's greengrocer, Paco, attended to his customers from a stand beside the entrance. While waiting in line, I would watch this young woman play mommy with my sons, and I would try to be understanding.

The wedges were fine with it. But the more upstanding neighborhood ladies who waited with me were clearly scandalized that I allowed this woman to put her lips and hands on my children.

"*No está limpia,*" (She's not clean,) one whispered to me once.

I had seen the disparaging remark coming for weeks and was prepared.

"*¡Se llama Dulcinea! ¡Y es impecable!*" (Her name is Sweetness! And she's impeccable!)—a line from *Don Quijote*.

No one got the joke.

Then one day it got serious. The woman, caught up in her mommy role, gave Wedge Two a whack on the behind for having hit Wedge One. It was a light whack, but a whack nonetheless, and Wedge Two, who took any scolding to heart, bolted from the plaza, furious, heading for the traffic-heavy road. I shot from my place in line, scooped up my son like a football, and carried him back to safety.

Reentering the plaza, I shouted at the woman.

"I'm the parent, not you! *¡Coño!*"

Having held my tongue for so long under the scrutiny of the *barrio*'s kangaroo court, now I had overdone it. The judgment-casters chimed in, pelting her with comments of their own. I had instigated a stoning. She was reduced to tears.

That night, I began to tell my half orange what happened, hoping for an empathetic ear. When I got to the part where the young woman would lift our boys onto her lap, my wife, normally the only *andaluza* to give me the benefit of the doubt as far as childrearing, popped her eyes wide and put her hands to her head.

"*¡Eres un tonto pelao!*" (You're a shorn fool!) she said. "*¡Si quieres jugar a santo de poca monta, hazlo contigo mismo, no con nuestros hijos!*" (If you want to play two-bit saint, do it with yourself, not with our sons!) She cast her eyes heavenward. "*¡Dios Mío! ¡No puedo confiar en él!*" (My God! I can't trust him!)

If my half orange had been in charge that morning, she would have bought the groceries elsewhere, outside of Madre de Dios, or would have said to the wedges, "Don't leave my side! Don't talk to anyone!"

That way of doing things, even if ultimately saving everyone a lot of trouble, was simply beyond me.

"Because you're vain and proud!" my half orange said.

Maybe so. Anyway, I had not learned my lesson—no maybes about that—because two weeks later, Madre de Dios's two-bit saint was back in top form.

An older woman I had never laid eyes on before but who must have seen me and the wedges many times, sticking out in Madre de Dios like a three-pronged sore thumb, approached us carrying a bulky black garbage bag. She explained that she was on her way to a secondhand shop to get rid of a couple of things but that it actually broke her heart to see them put up for sale. Maybe my boys would like them? She undid the drawstring on the garbage bag and pulled out two stuffed animals as big as the wedges—a bumble bee with red and pink stripes and a yellow frog in an elegant gray suit. Overjoyed, the wedges pulled them down into the double stroller, creating a pile of kid-sized bodies, half animate, half-inanimate, intertwined in a collective hug.

"They still have the store tags," said the woman, in case I continued to harbor doubts.

I harbored some—namely how I was going to explain this to my *sevillana*. Such a situation would never have happened to her. Sevillians, after getting used to the presence of a *guiri*, will take liberties with him, giving in to impulses both generous and stingy that they suppress around the people they've spent their whole lives among. They can be bossy, overly protective, sometimes cruel, but mostly kind, saying whatever occurs to them. Basically, they're more themselves.

Clearly this woman felt fantastic about what she'd done, and I didn't want to be *un aguafiestas* (to rain on her parade), so I kept my reservations to myself, accepting her gift, even thanking her like she was some kind of out-of-season Santa Claus.

By the time we got home, the new family additions had names: Pinky and Froggy.

The dreaded moment came at 3 p.m. when my half orange walked in the door from work. She immediately saw that we were not alone.

"And this?" she said, stopping in her tracks before the happy quartet sharing the sitting-room sofa, watching *Pocoyo* (Little Me) on the *caja tonta* (boob tube).

I had toyed with the idea of concocting some tale, telling her that we had gotten Pinky and Froggy in some grand opening giveaway, or thanks to a bank promotion, or won them in a street carnival a few neighborhoods away, but in the end I opted for the truth.

"The sweetest old lady gave them to us, wrapped in plastic, with the store tags still on—"

"*¡Y un cuerno!*" (And a horn!)—the kind that protrudes from a man's groin.

She went to the kitchen, yanked a garbage bag out of the box beneath the sink, and returned to the living room on a beeline for Pinky and Froggy, the only ones who did not seem disconcerted.

"No need to go overboard," I said.

"Overboard? You think so?" she said. "What would your mother do?"

She stuffed Pinky and Froggy into the garbage bag, pulled the drawstring tight, and brought the bag to the front door to take down with the garbage.

"*¡Mamiii! ¡Mamiii! ¡Nooo!*" the wedges cried out.

"Blame your father!" she shouted back.

I slipped out the door, off to work, aware that my presence would only prolong the strife. I should have known better than to accept that woman's gift. I should have known that my half orange would not be convinced.

Maybe she was Mother of God's only true saint and I was her cross, too full of myself to say no.

Later that week, walking through the makeshift Saturday flea market nearby, I encountered Pinky and Froggy propped up on a dirty blanket, a couple hundred feet from where the woman had given them to us. Beside them on the sidewalk sat a gypsy with his knees pulled to his chest and a cup of change at his bare feet. Clearly

Pinky and Froggy had been the prize find of that week's garbage picking.

I imagined our out-of-season Santa Claus seeing them.

"It was my wife's decision. She's *sevillana*," I would say if we ever crossed paths again.

DIPPING MY TOE IN

An hour before kickoff and I had yet to find my glasses.
"I'm going to get a headache," I complained to my half orange. "If people in this city didn't demand so many explanations from me, I'd call Javier right now and tell him something came up and I can't go."

"*Eres un miope en tó, chiquillo,*" (You're near-sighted in everything, kiddo,) she replied. In Spanish, or at least *andalú*, near-sighted also means shortsighted.

"Just wear these," she added.

They were her old glasses. When I propped them on the bridge of my nose, one of the lenses fell out. I picked it up off the floor, replaced it, and adjusted the frame on my face. Suddenly the world came into focus. Only the color of the frames put me off: bright red.

"Consider it a sign," she said.

White and bright red are the team colors of Sevilla Fútbol Club, whose stadium, Ramón Sánchez-Pizjuán, I would be heading to in a minute to see my first live professional soccer match.

Soccer is no trivial matter in Seville, which I had known upon arriving to the city, and so I had been careful, even reluctant, about choosing a favorite team.

Before Sevilla FC home games, I had often waded wide-eyed through the frothy red sea of fans, against the tide, moving away from the stadium on my return from work while everyone else converged on it. Then, from my sixth-floor landing, I would look back and see the stadium oval making an O at the sky, topped with a bubble of hazy blueish light. Soon I would hear the team anthem, sung by the crowd. For the next two hours, the hysteria after goals and the collective *oof*s after missed chances would arrive an instant later over the rooftops to mix with the resounding reactions of my fellow residents following the game on radio or TV.

If I hadn't learned to love baseball in the late '70s by rooting for the perennially cellar-dwelling New York Mets, I probably would have aligned my sympathies with the neighborhood team. Instead I was drawn to their *eterno rival* on the other side of the city, Real Betis Balompié, which had been at the bottom of the standings since I arrived in Seville, even dropping to *Segunda División* for a couple of seasons. Not only did Betis need my support more, but their motto, "*¡Manque pierda!*" (Even in loss!), described true loyalty, while Sevilla FC's "*¡Nunca se rinde!*" (Never give up!) smacked of cliché.

For a few years, I remained resolutely on the fence. *No me mojé* (I didn't get wet), as Sevillians liked to say. When neighborhood men would ask my wedges the standard question, "*¿De qué equipo eres?*" (What team do you root for?)—it being clear that there were only two options—I would answer for the three of us, saying, "*Ambos.*" (Both.)

The response was almost always the same:

"*¡Eso no puede ser! El uno o el otro. Las cosas como son.*" (That can't be! One or the other. That's just how it is.)

Once, out of curiosity, I strapped the wedges into the double stroller and headed for Ramón Sánchez-Pizjuán Stadium on derby day. I'd heard that the die-hard Betis fans would be marching over three miles from their stadium to Sevilla FC's, singing the team anthem the whole way. This I had to see.

As we approached the stadium, the growing crowd kindly parted until we reached nearly the first row along the police-barricaded procession route. Then fortune smiled on us.

"Here they come!" cried the woman in front of us, raising her hands to her head. She turned to me, eyes as big as soccer balls. "They're savages! Get the kids out of here!"

Then she fled, allowing the wedges and me to take her place, where we saw the Béticos, *los verdiblancos* (the green and whites), pass by militantly but peacefully.

The hysteria of that Sevillista and her unfair accusation tipped me toward green and white for good. It helped that Betis lost that derby by the scandalous score of 5-1.

But the day I wore my wife's bright red eyeglasses to my first pro soccer match, I still hadn't committed to one team or the other, which was probably why my student Javier had decided to invite me to a game, hoping to convert me to the one true faith through a full immersion baptism.

Javier's house, just five minutes away, was exactly eleven blocks from Ramón Sánchez-Pizjuán Stadium's eastern plaza. He was waiting for me on his doorstep, holding a thermal bag that perfectly matched the color of my glasses.

"Submarine sandwiches for half-time," he said.

"Thanks," I said. "But I just had dinner."

"You just had dinner? *Now*?"

Clearly Spaniards, not *estadounidenses*, ate at funny times, but, as a guest, I kept that to myself.

Javier insisted. "Going to a soccer match with your submarine sandwich is a time-honored tradition in Spain."

"Don't worry," I said. "I'll work up an appetite with my cheering."

How was it possible that my half orange had not warned me about *el momento bocadillo* (the submarine sandwich moment), the Spanish equivalent to the seventh-inning stretch—except that during this break you weighed yourself down with a massive cold-cut hero instead of lightening your load on a trip to the toilet. Incredible that, after five years together, my wife still failed to understand the delicacy of my digestive system. As if the commotion and excitement of the match would not be enough to upset my regularity, on top of that I would have to eat a foot-long sandwich an hour before going to sleep? Well, if she had to suffer the consequences of my gastric distress beneath the sheets that night, she'd get what she deserved.

As Javier and I headed off, I noticed the packs of out-of-towners—"the Bridge and Tunnel Crowd," they would be called in New York—who had parked on the outskirts of the neighborhood and were now enjoying the stroll to hallowed ground with their red and white scarves wrapped around their wrists like oversized identity bracelets. At least until the game was over, these yokels would have a rightful claim to the city.

Being a Bridge and Tunnel guy myself, I remembered a time back in the '80s when my dad took me, my brother, and a college friend to a Mets game at Shea. We parked on the back streets of Flushing Meadows, Queens, so as not to have to pay the stadium's exorbitant parking fees. In fact, we parked so far away that we could not find the car after the game.

"Officer, have you seen a blue Toyota?" my dad asked a traffic cop.

"Yeah, pal," the cop responded. "More than a Jap mechanic."

We finally found it after circling the side streets for an hour. Then we got caught in a massive traffic jam on the way home. I had stopped going to pro sports events after that. Getting there and back was too much of a drag to even think about.

Seville is smaller, so Javier and I had it easy. Our approach to the stadium went, as the Spanish say, *sobre ruedas* (over wheels), until we hit the turnstiles. Then we got clotheslined.

Javier's friend's season pass would not let me through. We tried to solve the problem at the ticket office but needed his friend's help. Impossible. It was August, he was at the beach, and would not even pick up the phone.

"*Vaya putada,*" (What whorishness,) said Javier, then handed me his season pass, the submarine sandwiches, and insisted, in no uncertain terms, that I see the match without him.

Despite enjoying Javier's company, I was relieved to be alone. I don't like being a guest. Now I could take in the scene without having to be overly deferential. If I didn't want to eat my hero, for example, I wouldn't.

Once I found my seat, I was able to relax and get in the mindset. I knew Sevilla FC was playing a European Champions

League match against Hannover 96 to see who would advance to the group stage. I quickly got a bead on the German team's star midfielder, Jan Schlaudraff, because the fans around me began berating him for his baldness as he stretched along the sideline. Well, if baldness were a crime, then the home team president, José María del Nido (Joseph Mary of the Nest), deserved life imprisonment. From where I sat, I could see his shining dome nodding in the president's box. Come to think of it, most of the guys shaming Schlaudraff for his hair loss seemed to be suffering from the same condition.

The two guys in front of me made no attempt to conceal the spliff they were sharing. They'd exhale great clouds of smoke which blew backwards into my face before dispersing into the night air. I was grateful for the contact high, although it made me nostalgic for the odor of ballpark franks and hot pretzels and the sight of those high-stepping concessions guys, athletes in their own right, hefting their dripping, sudsy racks up and down the bleacher aisles, bellowing out, "Bee-uh hee-uh!"

When the first notes of the Sevilla FC anthem blasted tinnily from the stadium speakers, the fans' voices drowned it out with roaring, authentic music. Never before had I heard so many people sing so loudly in perfect unison. It brought to mind a Mass I had seen Pope John Paul II celebrate in Yankee Stadium in 1979, when I was twelve years old.

"Peace be with you," said the Superpontiff.

"And also with you!" responded fifty-five thousand believers, shaking the foundations.

With so many Sevillistas on their feet, swaying to their hymn, I went so far as to pray for world peace and prosperity. If the house of God was where spirit, faith, and longing resided, then clearly my prayer would be heard.

Perhaps I should have prayed for Sevilla FC. They blew a bunch of chances, while Hannover 96, clearly outplayed, scored on their only solid counterstrike. The final score meant that Sevilla FC had been eliminated from the competition. Even so, the fans took it in stride. Everybody exited the stadium with a sprightly step. Not a single bottleneck detained us—inconceivable in New York. And, best of all, no need to look for a blue Toyota.

Javier, who had watched the game from his living room couch, sent me a text reminding me to drop off his season pass. I remembered the subs and my heart sank. Should I throw mine in the trash? That would be unthinkable after such happy religious fervor. I looked around for a homeless person to palm mine off on, but no such luck.

In the end, at Javier's door, we coincided so much in our enthusiasm about Sevillian right-winger Jesús Navas' ability to shrug off defenders with his slashing speed that I forgot to return the thermal bag, and Javier forgot to ask me for it. I discovered it hanging from my arm when I got home, then crammed the whole thing in the fridge.

"How was the match?" my half orange called out from bed.

"A new experience," I replied.

"Did the lens fall out?" she asked.

I checked, and nearly poked my eye out.

"Yeah," I said. "And I have no idea where it is."

"The things that happen to you!" she said. "Were you able to see?"

I gave the question some thought.

"I would have enjoyed the match even if I'd been blind," I said.

The next day, before meeting Javier for English class and returning his thermal bag, I ate my chorizo sub. That was my way of getting wet.

(ALMOST) GONE WITH THE WIND

The first time I took my half orange to the United States, she was six months pregnant. As soon as we got off the plane, she rushed to the restrooms and came back saying that they were "*fuera de servicio*" (out of order). I led her to some others, but she emerged saying the same. When it happened a third time, I finally asked her what exactly "*fuera de servicio*" meant.

"All the toilets are filled up almost to the top with water," she said.

"Ah," I said, relieved. "That's how toilets are in my country." (The Spanish variety are more like funnels than bowls, with only the tapered bottom covered with water.)

Her eyes opened wide.

"And if I fall in?"

"Don't worry," I said, placing my hand on her belly. "With this, you won't fit through."

Five minutes later, pleased to have cleared our first cultural hurdle unscathed, we set off to pick up our luggage. There, the requisite grumpy Customs guard made a disdaining gesture to the stowaway bulging from beneath my half orange's dress and asked her how far along she was. My half orange, thrilled to have understood the question in English, did not catch the innuendo.

After explaining to her that the guard suspected that the reason for her visit was to give birth in the States and therefore guarantee the baby's US citizenship, my *sevillana* looked perplexed for a moment, then looked back at the guard, staring hard.

"*Pero es un chino,*" (But he's Chinese,) she said.

Normally, I would have said to her that perhaps in Seville you could get away with calling all East Asians Chinese, but in the United States you risked summary excommunication. In this case, however, I only used one of her favorite adages, applicable to any and all exclusive clubs: "*El último mono es el peor al siguiente en la fila.*" (The last monkey in is the worst to the next in line.)

With our luggage retrieved and piled on carts, we finally made it past Customs, where my brother was waiting for us, as long and lanky as ever.

"How tall!" said my wife. "What big feet!"

She would say the same thing about my father and almost all of my friends. The United States was the nation of the physically big: the people, the cars, the houses, the clothes, the take-out coffees—everything, absolutely everything, was oversized. The cliché could not have been truer. I hadn't realized it when living here. After two years away, I got the sense that my half orange and I were about to be swallowed whole. In Seville, there was only one physical thing that existed on such a scale: the heat—not just big, but crushing.

The airport had suffocated us both, but once let loose inside the country, my wife claimed to feel like "*una foca*" (a seal)—the Spanish equivalent of "a fat cow"—teetering on the edge of a toilet yawning wide and filled to the brim. To me she appeared more like a balloon attached to earth by a tiny, invisible string, threatening to disappear into American magnitude and dimension.

For a woman who had always taken great delight in being tiny but resolute, yet who, in those weeks of heightened gestation, was getting visibly larger every day, it was a boost to her self-esteem that her surroundings had blown up in size much more than she had. You had to see her, as happy as a pair of clicking castanets, the day we went to buy her some snow boots and found her size in the kids' section.

Only a day later she would say to me, "Walking over the snow when you're six months pregnant is like walking through the sands of the desert with a broken leg."

But she would remain a good sport to the end. I managed to convince her to walk halfway across the Brooklyn Bridge with me while it was sprinkling freezing rain. She panted up the whole incline, leaning on my arm. When we finally reached the peak of the span, she admitted it had been worth it. There we hung, suspended, exhilarated, over the city in a web of steel cables, girders, and beams, with traffic roaring beneath our feet and the frigid, spitting wind in our faces. We looked back at the cityscape lit up like thousands of April Fair *portadas*.

We spent most of the ten-day trip in North Sutton, New Hampshire—right in the heart of the state's snow belt—where my parents had retired after almost forty years on Staten Island. My half orange was living true winter for the first time in her life. Previously, she had only ever seen snow on a ski slope in Granada and the majority of it had been artificial. She needed, I felt, to experience the authentic article in all its natural and invigorating glory, and the most fitting way to achieve that would be to hit her smack in the *culo* (butt) with a snowball when she least expected it.

Night had fallen and the moon was full when I found the opportune moment to carry out my plan. Flurries had descended during the day, but my half orange, Sevillian to the bone, had dressed for a blizzard. With so many layers of clothing, she could not even press her arms to her sides. As if that and her already increased size were not enough, she had just stuffed herself with my mother's homemade snowball cookies and pumpkin bread. A fat target, if there ever was one.

My first toss hit home, but her cushion of clothes kept her oblivious. I crouched down for more ammo and packed it tight. When I stood to set my sights on her again, I was surprised to see how tiny she'd become. How had she gotten so far away? Out there in front of me, she looked like an astronaut floating in space, white space. I let the snowball drop and ran to catch up to her before she vanished, taking with her our stowaway, still safely and snugly concealed.

THE LAST OF THE *SEVILLANAS*

We returned to the States again in early summer, with the New Hampshire countryside at its greenest possible exuberance. One morning while eating breakfast with my mother, I spotted a mama bear and two cubs sprinting across the backyard vegetable garden, taking with them the fence of stakes and strings, which bounced and tumbled along behind them like cans attached to the car of newlyweds. Their velocity was astonishing as they disappeared into the forest on the other side of the lawn, their thick bodies folding and extending in strides as rapid as the beating of wings.

"God almighty," I said, returning to my granola.

My mom was calmly sipping her tea.

"They're as afraid of us as we are of them," she said.

"As afraid as you are or as afraid as I am?" I asked.

"I respect them more than fear them," she said, getting up to give a demonstration. "If you come across one, under no circumstances should you try to escape, especially if it's a mama bear with her cubs, because you haven't got a chance. The trick is to stay exactly where you are and make yourself as big as possible." She raised her arms above her head. Even on tiptoes, she seemed a trifling thing for a bear. "And wait until it leaves."

"Dragging you kicking and screaming to its lair," I said.

"Bears don't eat meat. They live off berries and ants."

"Right, an animal that big eats like a bird."

"I'm more careful with the snapping turtles," she said. "In spring, they come up from the stream bed to lay and bury their eggs. They're extremely quick when they turn to face a threat. If they get a hold of your finger, the only way to make them let go is to cut off their heads."

There were also moose that, according to my mother, were as aggressive and surprisingly agile as bears when caught off guard in their territory, and coyotes that moved in packs and howled at the moon, and, perhaps most dangerous of all, backwoods country folk who did not take kindly to anyone, man or beast, trespassing on their property. It was not uncommon in the weekly papers for a photo to appear of a family posing with a rifle, no doubt still smoking, and a bear dead at their feet that they found nosing around their compost pit.

To me, the Andalusian wilderness was relatively tame. What once was wild now existed under control, on *fincas* (ranches) or as part of the folklore, and presented hardly any danger to anyone except perhaps a few brave and extremely well-trained performance artists in the bullring. On the other hand, across vast stretches of the United States, the wilds continued to be present in daily life, in their primal state.

To Spaniards who challenged me on this point, I would bring up two of my favorite books: *Don Quixote*, written by Miguel de Cervantes in the early sixteen hundreds about a loony gentleman knight who invented enemies, like windmills, and confronted them to be able to feel like the heroes he had read about in books; and *The Last of the Mohicans*, written over two hundred years later by the *estadounidense* James Fenimore Cooper, about three renegade warriors who behaved according to the laws of nature, not of man, and who were surrounded on all sides by real enemies.

I liked the idea that my parents had bought seven acres of wild land so that their grandkids could run free on it. I wanted my children to know the new world as well as the old. That would be their privilege.

We were sleeping at my brother's house, about a hundred yards away from my parents' place if you passed through a dense stretch of forest, stepping over bear and coyote droppings, and crossed the stream on stepping stones, hoping that none of them was the shell of a ferocious turtle. You could also take what I as a kid would have called "the wussy way" by walking down my parents' long winding driveway, making a left on the road, and then another left up my brother's driveway. That took about ten minutes, and you would only have a few deer fly bites to show for it.

My half orange always insisted on taking the wussy way, and she walked it at a New Yorker's pace while holding Wedge One wrapped in one of her linen scarves to keep the vermin from feasting on him. At night, even when moon- or starlight guided our way, she simply refused to walk back from my parents' house without a flashlight.

"Forget about the flashlight," I said one night, as we were about to step outdoors after stuffing ourselves with my mother's prosciutto chicken. "You must *feel* the way with your feet. Like a Mohican."

"*¡Un mojón para ti!*" (A turd for you!) she responded. Playing the brute was one of her tactics to pluck up courage.

My mother turned to me, looking for a translation.

"She wants the flashlight," I said, "to make sure that we don't step in bear poo."

My mother, who appreciated her daughter-in-law much more than her son's infantile sense of humor, rolled her eyes and went for the flashlight.

"Do you want the bear bells too?" she called back. You attached them to your ankles, as if you were a Clydesdale in the Christmas ad, and supposedly the bears were scared off before you got within range for an attack.

"Don't worry," I replied. "My wife was born for this walk. She's Andalusian. She can sing."

Once we were properly equipped, I opened the door and pushed her outside as she hugged Wedge One against her bosom. Clouds and dense foliage blanketed the night sky.

"Look!" I said, pointing to the circle of light that the flashlight made on the gravel drive. "*Un lunar.*" (A polka dot.)

The word originates from *luna* (moon). It was all my wife needed to break into song.

"*¡Qué bonita está la noche con la luz de la linterna!*" (How beautiful is the night by the light of the flashlight!)

It was a variation on *Candela, Candela* (Campfire, Campfire), a standard on the pilgrimage to El Rocío, sung to keep spirits high when the wagon trains would stop for the night. As we walked, our cultures merged and we took on new roles. I was the errant knight escorting my Dulcinea safe and sound back home, and my half orange was the pioneer, defying the wilds of a new world, armed only with a flashlight and a song.

"*¡Linterna! ¡Linterna! ¡Cómo luce la linterna!*" (Flashlight! Flashlight! How the flashlight shines!)

XXL

In a photo my sister once sent me of my then seven-year-old niece, she was drinking a Coke at a firefighters' picnic on Staten Island. The twenty-ounce plastic cup completely blocked out her face. The image reminded me of that scene from *Conan the Destroyer*, when Arnold Schwarzenegger raises his sword on high and his entire head disappears behind his bicep.

On our trips back to the States, I marvel at my native country's size and scale, which I didn't comprehend before living abroad. My half orange, wedges, and I drive past single stores and strip malls bigger than villages that we pass through on our way to *Las Minas*. We do our shopping in carts that require more parking space than a Ford Ka, a car too small to even be marketed in the States. Many two-car garages could be converted into homes that would make an Andalusian family proud. Staten Islanders head to the Jersey Shore on twelve-lane expressways, migrating like wildebeests; Sevillians go to the beach on winding highways, traveling in single file like elephants.

I've got nothing against the physically large if it's practical and appropriate. If my half orange sits on a couch and her feet don't touch the floor, or if she has to climb into the guest bed rather than collapse into it, well, my compatriots are generally large, certainly much larger than she is, and this has to be taken into account when designing furniture.

On the other hand, there is US urban sprawl. In Seville, the wedges and I can do the daily errands while taking a neighborhood stroll. In a mile loop, we pass the bakery, the greengrocer's, the butcher's, the hardware store, the pharmacy, the bank, a couple of parks, and at least three schools. Meanwhile, in the land of Manifest Destiny, where the objective has almost always been to expand, if we want to hit so many different places, we have to get in and out of the car at least four times. On top of that, there's the distance driven. In my parents' part of New Hampshire, such a laborious round trip would cover about seven miles.

New York City is different, of course. There, people do their errands on foot but under pressure. In Seville, the crowded streets are social, almost festive. You can dilly and dally, stop to chat with a neighbor, or stare at the sky. In Manhattan, if you pause on a busy sidewalk to get your bearings, you end up pissing people off. I can recall being one of the hyper-accelerated go-getters, secretly wishing the meanderers would get bulldozed, punished for their lack of relentless direction.

Once, after seeing a music video set in New York City, my half orange blurted out, "What a shame! If we ever get to live in New York, I'll be too old to enjoy it."

"No," I replied. "You'll be too old to put up with it."

"C'mon," she said. "Wouldn't you want to live in New York again?"

"Not unless I made heaps of money doing what I absolutely love," I said.

When visiting my former city, I always make a point to enter the southern part of Central Park. There, I can relax and take it all in. The skyscrapers rise up along the border, yet I'm surrounded by hills, trees, winding paths, and a pond. It's in precisely this spot that the immensity of the urban center runs smack up against the abundance of America's wide-open spaces.

From this vantage, New York's bigness really is better because it stands at attention before a small patch of the natural vastness that inspired it. The gesture is bold but deferential. Too often my country's bigness seems grotesque, like one of those bucket-sized iced coffees from Dunkin' Donuts.

In Seville, the beers, although small, are cold, and the coffees, even smaller, are potent. I pass my day-to-day life in a city where the single skyscraper is as out of place as a bullring would be on Wall Street, and where the only public thoroughfare wide enough for twelve lanes of traffic is the Guadalquivir River. I buy in shops that have more space behind the counter than in front of it. In my neighborhood, people bring their groceries home in dolly carts, not the trunks of their SUVs. The unhurried steps of Sevillians obstruct me at times, it's true, but whenever I second-guess my steps, I don't feel at risk of being stampeded.

No offense against New York, but right now I prefer living on a human rather than a superhuman scale.

EYES TO SEE THE ORANGE TREES

When I first arrived in Seville in November of 2005, the city was preparing for Christmas. Orange trees on both sides of the main drag, Avenida de la Constitución, were weighed down with fruit that served extemporaneously as ornaments. The branches had been strung with starry blue lights. I thought of my grandfather growing up on a farm in Lithuania just before World War I getting only an orange for Christmas. His old man then cuffed him for complaining about Father Christmas's stinginess.

From scarcity to abundance in two generations.

After a couple of years, I stopped seeing the orange trees, or, rather, I saw them without seeing them. I did see the fallen oranges. The city variety, it turned out, were too bitter to eat. I worried that if the street sweepers did not come soon to remove them, the rats in Madre de Dios were going to be as numerous as the flies.

I remember when the sight of the white doves fluttering around the Seville Cathedral would soothe me with thoughts of world peace, Aphrodite, and the Holy Spirit. Too soon I began lumping the doves in with the pigeons: birds of a feather...rats with wings.

At one time, on my way back from work when Sevilla FC was playing at home, I would pass the multitude of fans with their puffed-out chests converging on Ramón Sánchez-Pizjuán Stadium and feel a surge of pride that I lived in a city where the pro sports arenas were surrounded by schools, homes, and churches. But once settled into a routine, I began cursing the traffic jams and lack of parking around my building, knowing that the next day the side streets would stink of urine.

Once upon a time, when Sevillians had talked at the tops of their voices and gesticulated furiously about the most mundane

aspects of their lives, I had marveled at their impulsiveness and passion. I had tuned in my ear, ready to lap up the music of the city, even the most grating, disharmonious composition of notes. As time passed, when I would see one Sevillian venting to another, I would think, *It's as though every pimple in their nether regions was a looming volcano about to erupt and bury the city.* If I was in a long supermarket line or on a slow city bus, and some local began to yammer on to me about people's general incompetence, I'd deflect the assault by saying, "Sorry, I don't understand," then snicker inwardly when the snubbed Sevillian thought I meant the language.

I missed my eyes of surprise, before prejudices and haste had tarnished my adoptive city. Newcomers supposedly needed time to glimpse, sniff out, and savor the truth, but my senses had seemed far more attuned just after arriving to Seville.

My first time passing the Real Alcázar, I had to lay my hands on the walls to make sure those enormous blocks of stone were not the fiber-reinforced gypsum plaster of the Cinderella Castle in Disneyland. Soon enough I went from awestruck wonder to passing the palace walls with my head bent, moving right along so that the gypsy women who loitered there did not mistake me for a tourist and try to sell me a sprig of rosemary for luck.

I had once meandered the maze of ancient masonry between Plaza Alfalfa and Puerta de la Carne, not caring if those echoing alleyways became my prison and I, a Sevillian Sisyphus, was condemned to spend eternity wearing down cobblestones already scuffed smooth by centuries of use. Now I walked the same stretch focused only on not getting sideswiped by a cab as I circumnavigated the tourists clogging up the sidewalks consulting their phones and fold-out maps.

On trips to the city center, I used to see the ruin of the Roman aqueduct from the window of the bus and wonder if Apostle Paul had ever blessed the water that ran its course. Then I began catching that bus on the way home from work. Once crammed in with other commuters, if I happened to look up from my reading to peer out the window, the aqueduct was nothing more than the marker that we had finally left behind the congestion of downtown.

This change in my perspective only hit me after taking my half orange to New York for our honeymoon. We were on the train back to New Hampshire when I asked her, "Tell me your three favorite things about the city."

She did not have to think for long.

"The snow, the Christmas shoppers, and the squirrels that ate out of my hand in Battery Park," she said.

When I lived in New York, the snow dragged out my daily commute even more, the throngs of Christmas shoppers would block my way as I rushed to arrive on time to class, and on Staten Island the squirrels were noxious neighborhood pests that snuck into attics and nested there, disrupting the homeowners' sleep. My half orange had chosen as her New York highlights three things that had once been obstacles and threats to my good spirits.

Thanks to her, I began to recall how the snow can transform a roaring and hostile metropolis into a blissfully hibernating beast; that the holiday shoppers, with their brightly colored bags and leisurely pace, add a festive touch to a city normally consumed by greed and competitiveness; and that the squirrels, as long as they stay in the parks, remind humans that nature and civilization, even civilization at its most extreme, can coexist without one threatening the other with extinction.

We must preserve our eyes to see the orange trees.

THE WEDGES

ACID TEST

Wedge One, at two years old, once caught the attention of a teenager passing in front of our building.

"What a beautiful little girl!" she exclaimed.

"Boy," I shot back.

As was usually the case with young ladies from Madre de Dios, she was not easily cowed.

"Well, there are pink hearts on his T-shirt," she responded. The observation was impossible to deny. My half orange had dressed him. When the girl was out of sight, I squatted down, removed the T-shirt, and put it back on inside out.

When we returned home, my wife got one look at him and asked, "What's up with his shirt?"

"Someone thought he was a girl," I said, indignant.

Boy, did my half orange have a laugh at my expense.

Every day it seems clearer to me that there are three sure acid tests to finding out if you really know yourself: live abroad, get married, and have kids. I said my marital vows in my half orange's homeland, before a judge whose language I could not yet understand, with my then four-month-old sitting on my knee. The results have shown me that I still have quite a ways to go before I become the man without prejudices or hang-ups that I thought I was before the onset of the revolution.

I once said with pride that, if I ever had a son, I'd have him study ballet. He would grow up admiring Margot Fonteyn, Martha Graham, and Alicia Alonso as much as Muhammad Ali, Michael Jordan, and Joe DiMaggio. But now that my male progeny is no longer hypothetical, I prefer that they one day play basketball or soccer, or, if they choose dance, then hip-hop or flamenco. I'm also glad they enjoyed *Chitty Chitty Bang Bang* more than *The Sound of Music*, although I introduced them to both.

Having a wife who is not only Andalusian but also New Age-y in her tastes at least keeps me in a healthy state of self-questioning. I've been forced to get used to the fact that our apartment often resembles a hybrid between an Andalusian Eden and a hippie commune, with our Mediterranean earth mother presiding over the peace, love, and grooviness, just a few skimpy garments away from being *como su madre la trajo al mundo* (as her mother brought her into the world).

During the early years, I would answer the call of nature with the bathroom door wide open. My diaper-clad wedges would be beside me floating paper boats in the bidet, and my half orange, recently emerged from the shower, would be rubbing her hot, damp body with oil. If only there were a way to find a moment alone with the woman! Later in the evening, we'd all end up falling asleep in one big heap on the marital bed. I'd have to wait until my sons were sound asleep before carrying them to their own beds. By then my half orange would be out for the night, too. Sometimes it was all just too much to bear.

"*¡Qué churrita más blanquita! ¡Parece un Pictolín!*" (What a weenie most white! It looks like a Jolly Rancher!) said my half orange once while changing Wedge Two.

"Good God!" I shouted from the kitchen. "I'm trying to have a snack!"

She emerged from the wedges' room with her hands on her hips.

"What's the problem?"

"Such comparisons, if you insist on making them, should refer to your husband's anatomy, not your son's. And for God's sake, lower your voice. The walls are thin."

"I wouldn't describe yours as a Jolly Rancher exactly, but rather—"

I shut my eyes and covered my ears.

To her, not only am I old-fashioned, but also a prude—and my shortcomings don't stop there.

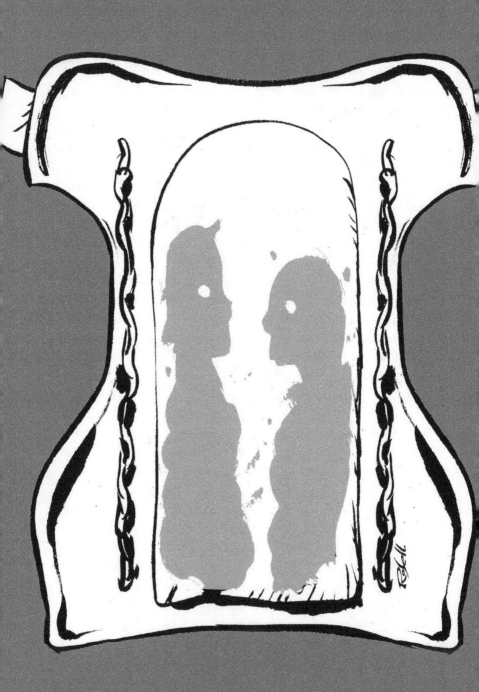

According to the norms of social behavior in Seville, a kiss on each cheek is given to members of the opposite sex when you are introduced. Pandemics aside, this custom is risky, especially if the woman has sex appeal. What happens if upon switching cheeks we accidentally Eskimo kiss? Or, if in a moment of lunacy, I sink my teeth into her neck?

The kind of light finger squeeze used in my homeland when men and women meet, holding our heads back as if afraid our breath might stink, squares better with my innate and cultural temperament. Nonetheless, the double kiss quickly became instinct, and I continue to employ it back in the States. As a rule, the women recoil and hang on desperately to their purses.

At least this proves I'm not the only skeptic. My countrywomen seem to distrust it more than I do.

But what about my discomfort when the traditional gender lines get blurred, as though I were the one wearing heart-covered clothes? The five brothers who run my local greengrocer's have come to address me as "*mi alma*" (my soul). They're burly country boys and die-hard Betis supporters, so I doubt I have anything to worry about, but you never know. Why can't they call me *campeón* (champion) or *fenómeno* (phenomenon)?

Then there's my Spanish brother-in-law. I know that his being a hairdresser shouldn't put me on guard, yet there it is in the back of my mind. He goes out of his way to share the best of his culture with me: the wine, the gastronomy, the bullfighting (i.e., gorgeous guys in tight, spangly pants). In 2005, Spain became the third country in the world to legalize same-sex marriages. One day my brother-in-law began to go on about the extravagant wedding that his two buddies were planning, and I prayed that he wouldn't ask me to come along as his guest. I'm trying to be honest here. I just did not want to go to a gay wedding accompanied by a hairdresser, even if he does look like Super Mario—which I realize we can't draw any conclusions from either.

What's happened to me? I once prided myself on being a paragon of social justice and a fervent advocate of marginalized peoples and perspectives. Who is this person having these thoughts, and perhaps even letting them condition his behavior?

Until recently, I was even squeamish about kissing the wedges. Fathers and sons just don't kiss in the Irish Catholic culture I was raised in. As far as physical contact, pats on the back and wrestling around on the floor are about the only things that come naturally to me. My half orange and my New York friend Gabriel— of Sicilian and Puerto Rican roots—finally convinced me that I had to overcome my cultural complexes in this respect. So one day on the way out the door, I bent down to show Wedge One the manly way to do it, but he beat me to the punch, planting the kiss directly on my lips.

I staggered out of the apartment as if I'd been blindsided by some secret crush.

SEX IN SEVILLE

Sexo en Nueva York, **the Spanish title for the TV series** *Sex and the City,* has always sounded to me like an anthropological study.

"Is it true that *Sexo en Nueva York* was based on a newspaper column?" my half orange asked one morning with the wedges still in bed.

I did not even peer up from my laptop. My wife loves to chat before the kids wake up. I love to work. The early morning hours are the most tranquil time of day and I always try to make the most of them.

"Was the star of the series real or a fictional character?" she persisted.

I held off answering in hopes that she would catch the hint.

"Are you listening to me?" she asked.

I pressed Ctrl+S and finally looked up.

"I only ever read the column two or three times," I said. "And I never saw the TV series. As far as whether it was based in reality or fiction, I always got the impression that, instead of the actresses playing the roles of real New Yorkers, real New Yorkers, crazy about the series, began to play the roles of the actresses. What a shame that only the superficial side of my culture gets exported to this country."

"I'm not surprised that you don't approve of it. It's very feminist. You wouldn't see its merits."

"Darling," I said, "could we postpone this conversation to another moment?"

"Always the same," she said. "Eating breakfast every morning with a slab of marble sitting across from me."

"Shh!" I said, gesturing towards the wedges' room.

"And now he tells me to shut up," she said.

"Fine." I closed my laptop, ready to wade into the thick of it. "You want to chat? Agreed, but no mincing words. The first time I entered your apartment and saw the *Sexo en Nueva York* DVDs stacked beneath your TV—let's just say that it wasn't a point in your favor."

"Would you have preferred a TV series about a cloistered convent?"

"Thank God it was a false alarm. No doubt the series is nonsense, but harmless in your case because you were sensibly raised."

"Nonsense, you say. Well, I say hilarious, with an admirable underlying message. There's one absolutely brilliant episode…" The juggernaut was rolling now, no stopping it. "One of the main characters, who loves sex, finally finds the perfect man: handsome, respectful, intelligent, romantic, rich. She tries to control herself and not have sex with him right away and ruin it, like she's done so many times before. Finally, the big night arrives. It's a dream come true for her, you know? The foreplay is perfect, prolonged, magical. She can't resist anymore. Breathless, she says. 'Now! Put it in!' And he says, 'It's in.' She opens her eyes, terrified. 'It's in? Really?'" My half orange held up her pinky. "A penis like this. Poor girl. Spent the whole next day crying."

"So what's the admirable underlying message?" I asked. "That your man has to be well-hung?"

"Men eat with their eyes," she said. "Why can't women?"

"So let's get this straight," I said. "I'm supposed to believe that you would have left me if I didn't have a penis big enough to satisfy you."

She pondered this.

"Aww, come off it," I said. "Maybe US women take the role of sexually liberated and modern female seriously. But not you old-world women. An *andaluza* understands perfectly what's truly important."

"In other words, sex isn't very important to you?" she said. "If I decided to live a life of celibacy with you, you wouldn't have any problem with that?"

I stood to wash the dishes. The roar of the butane water heater sometimes helped me think.

My half orange and I tended to spend more time washing dishes than eating off them. We refrained from buying a dishwasher for fear that the novelty and convenience of such an appliance would serve as irresistible stimulus to redo the entire kitchen, a luxury that we could in no way afford. Besides, the remodeling work would have been a *coñazo* (an enormous *coño*), depriving me of the meager moments of peace and quiet that family life allowed me.

Having bolstered my argument with a bit of housework, I shut off the faucet. The water heater went quiet, as though to give me the floor.

"What I'm trying to say, *cariño*, is that, although I don't want to live like a priest or to live with a nun, I'm glad to know that my wife was raised in an environment not completely devoid of traditional values."

My half orange was in the kitchen now too, picking through the hamper of dirty laundry. Filling the drum of a clothes washer with the infinity of tiny pants, socks, and bodysuits of pap-eating, diaper-wearing wedges, with the prospect of having to hang it all out to dry later, is an even more oppressive chore than washing dishes, but it only seemed to sharpen my wife's argumentative skills.

"By 'traditional,' I guess you mean chauvinist?" she said. "For instance, if a woman's husband has a penis the size of a shrimp, she has to endure it with a nightly performance. But if her husband has sex outside the relationship in order to satisfy his so-called virility, then she's to blame for not properly serving him."

"Do you know why there are so many divorces in the Western world?" I said.

"Because of TV series like *Sexo en Nueva York*," she replied. "*¡Bravo!*"

"Just listen to me," I said, throwing the mildewy dishrag in with the poo-stained clothes. "The spirit of the times tries to convince us that if we're not banging away at our romantic partners like rabbits in a cage, then our future together is bleak and we have to go in search of—"

"Orgasms."

"Exactly! What horseshit, no? You know as well as I do that couples go through stages. An excess of sex in a relationship can very well be a sign that it's an empty one. If the sex in a relationship isn't a nightly or even weekly occurrence, perhaps that means the love is fed by a wide variety of sources."

"You're aware, of course," she said, looking up, "that the exact same logic is used to explain why, in many supposedly fulfilling relationships, the man has his piece on the side. And when he's caught, he justifies himself by saying, 'It was just sex.' Would that response reassure you if you caught me with a lover?"

The drum of the washing machine was still far from filled.

I looked again toward the wedges' bedroom. So much talk about sex was making me lose my appetite for work. I stretched to get my blood flowing and rolled my head from side to side.

"Oof, *cariño*," I said. "Got a crick in my neck. Since the kids are still asleep, put the laundry aside for a moment and come help me loosen up."

"Ah! So you want to behave like a superficial New Yorker on the *caja tonta*. Well, I'm in the mood for a relationship fed by—"

In that moment, a nerve-jangling scream broke the glorious silence of the morning, the scream of a wedge with hunger pains, and a moment later, the whimpering cries of the other.

As my half orange moved briskly into action, I called out after her.

"If the characters of *Sexo en Nueva York* had been real, their sex would have produced children!"

YES!

Wedge One, at just over sixteen months old, added a new word to his English vocabulary: "Yes." It sank in during the ten celebratory seconds after Spanish soccer player Carles Puyol's header defeated Germany in the semifinals of the 2010 World Cup. As if it had not been strange enough for Wedge One to see me spending so much time squirming and sweating before the TV, not paying the slightest attention either to him, his fellow wedge, or the half orange in charge of us all, he had to watch his normally stoic dad jump up from the sofa, lift his arms in the air, and shout, "Yes! Yes! Yes!"

The poor guy had only ever heard me emphasize the opposite.

Four days later, I saw the final against Holland at Quique's place. Quique worked construction with Paco, who came over with his older son and a friend. Meanwhile, the wives were downstairs in the makeshift plaza below, watching the littler kids play.

The game against Holland was another nail-biter. While Puyol had scored the semifinal's only goal with seventeen minutes remaining, the final went scoreless well into overtime and looked like it would be resolved by a penalty shootout.

We had been in front of the TV for over two hours, night had fallen, and Quique's wife and daughters, six and two, were still in the street.

"Don't you think it's about time they came up?" I said.

Quique swatted the idea out of the air.

"We've only won when they haven't been home. If they come up now, our run is over," he said.

Just then, Jesús Navas got the ball in Dutch territory, sprinted along the right sideline, and cut toward midfield into a pack of Dutch players. Somehow, Andrés Iniesta got possession of the ball and heel-tapped it to Cesc Fàbregas, who passed back to Navas, who connected with Fernando Torres on the left side. A Dutch defender deflected Torres' center pass. Fàbregas got hold of it and threaded three Dutch players to find Iniesta wide open inside the area. Iniesta used his cannon of a right foot to score—as Fernando Torres would later put it—"*el gol de todos*" (everyone's goal).

A short while later, after screaming my head off and hopping around the living room in a pack with everyone, arms around each other, I stumbled back downstairs and into my apartment, hoarse and still euphoric.

My half orange got one look at me and froze.

"Why are you so flushed?" she said.

"Flushed?" I said. "Am I flushed? Your country just won the World Cup."

I looked in the hall mirror and was momentarily shocked. Then I remembered I had painted a Spanish flag, *la rojigualda* (the red and yellow), on each cheek at the suggestion of Paco's son. The sweat and nervous tension had made the paint run.

"That's just your national colors coursing through my veins," I said.

I love sports but avoid watching my favorite teams because I can't stand having my mood at the mercy of factors so completely out of my control. I make exceptions only in special cases.

In Spain, during the 2010 World Cup, network TV became a source of inspiration because every time the national team played—barring their opening loss against Switzerland—they perfectly executed a style of soccer, that, when all its virtues were displayed, kept you on the edge of your seat, mouth open in awe for ninety minutes (and, if you were lucky, for thirty minutes of overtime, too).

Thanks to this new style and, of course, guts, passion, stick-to-itiveness, unity, and sangfroid, *La Roja* had *hecho historia* (made history). Spanish journalists tossed that term around for weeks, which got me thinking about what exactly it meant to be present at the making of history. When recalling the assassination of a president, or a terrorist attack on the scale of 9/11 or the Madrid rail

bombings, or the declaration of war, most of us begin by saying where we were in the moment we found out, as if our principal objective were to put distance between ourselves and the unfortunate event.

But there's another type of historic moment that's an honor to be present at. I would have liked to be present at the fall of the Berlin Wall, at Spain's nonviolent transition to democracy, at Muhammad Ali's title fights against George Foreman and Joe Frazier, at all the opening nights of the New York City Ballet when George Balanchine was still directing the company, and at Barack Obama's ascent and triumph in US politics. Except for this last historic feat, I either had not been born yet or was not old enough to appreciate the significance of what was happening. I missed out on Obamamania because I was in Spain, but being present at the rise of *La Roja* almost compensated, because the phenomenon of *La Roja* was about more than just sports, just like Obama was about more than just politics.

Spain's national team had its run of glory from 2008 to 2012, just as the bottom dropped out of the Spanish economy after twenty years of dizzying economic growth. While Spanish citizens were coming to grips with just how corrupt, poorly run, and hopelessly in debt their country was, as they watched their politicians, bankers, and union leaders go on living like kings at the expense of the state after having scammed those they were supposed to serve, while social welfare programs were being radically cut just when they were most needed, while the rescued banks were evicting families and senior citizens from their homes for not being able to pay the mortgages that these same banks had greedily encouraged them to accept—and to add on a car and a luxury vacation too!—, there was *La Roja* taking down European economic powerhouses like Germany and Holland with a style of play known as "tiki-taka," which depended on cool heads, tactical precision, and teamwork ("everyone's goal," as Fernando Torres so accurately put it). *La Roja* had made manifest, at a popular level that only world-class sports, Top 40 music, and the Hollywood star system could approach, that

Spain had it in her to triumph in the most selfless, edifying, and thus satisfying of ways.

While *estadounidenses* tend to name ourselves world champions in sports we invented, *La Roja* triumphed internationally in a sport that it *re-invented*. The matches against Germany and Holland instilled in me the yearning to do something important with my life; surely I was not alone in this.

After washing the traces of *la rojigualda* from my face, I tried to return to earth by throwing myself into domestic tasks. While doing the dishes, I could not help peeking out occasionally to see the postgame interviews. I was standing next to my half orange in the living room when I saw *el beso del Mundial* (the World Cup kiss).

Ten million people, one quarter of the Spanish population, were watching when Sara Carbonero, smoldering before the camera, the meaning of life seeming to swirl behind her hypnotic, impossibly green eyes, interviewed her rumored boyfriend, Iker Casillas, Spain's star goalkeeper and the team captain. He began to thank his parents, his family; he looked at her meaningfully, then paused, overcome with emotion.

"Don't worry," she said, jumping in. "We'll see some highlights."

Casillas, with his infallible, game-saving instincts, pulled her into him, kissed her hard on the lips, then released her.

"*Me voy,*" (I'm out of here,) he said, then slipped out of view.

Left alone on the screen, Carbonero's previously imperturbable features, an ode to Mediterranean serenity, went completely to pieces.

"*Madre mía!*" she said and hid behind her lush curtain of hair.

The camera cut to the anchor, who, speaking for all of us, blurted out, "Casillas! What a great captain!"

I was so impressed by Iker's *pronto* that I swooped down and kissed my wife the same way. Walking back to the kitchen, I almost fell over Wedge One zipping around the house on his scooter.

"Yes! Yes! Yes!" I said, staring at my son so the word would sink in.

SEVILLITY

Every morning in front of our building, at least one brand-new, original work of canine art was lying in wait to catch my wedges and me off guard. When the wedges were tiny, we would never leave the apartment without a plentiful supply of wet wipes, as much for accidents involving our shoe bottoms and the stroller wheels as for those involving the wedges' rear ends. My friend Gabriel and his wife Kelly, who lived in a much cleaner part of the city, were nonetheless so impressed by the exhibition of canine creations that, once back home, they would point to the New York variety and exclaim, "Look, it's a Seville!" To grate on boosterish Sevillians, I sometimes joke that the tourist office should print a postcard of its most ubiquitous and stalwart monument with the slogan *"Pisa Sevilla"* (Set Foot in Seville).

Yet a lesson festered beneath this filth. One morning in the park, while pushing the wedges on the swings, I saw a guy looking the other way while his dog squatted in the center of the walking path. The dog finished his business and began sniffing around as the owner ignored the output, bending down to pick up something else. In Seville, civic-mindedness is equivalent to meddling in government affairs. Pick a piece of litter up from the ground and people peg you as some kind of anal apparatchik. Even so, the man stood peering over his shoulder, as if scanning the scene for witnesses. Our eyes met, and I shook my head in disgust.

Sometimes instant chemistry springs up between people, chemistry for conflict. As he stepped out smartly in my direction, still holding whatever he had picked up, I imagined his mind racing, preparing his opening sally against my *guiri* scorn. He was way wrong if he thought he could put me in my place on this one. Even before settling down in Madre de Dios, I had been planning my defense of the public thoroughfare. Finally, with this hothead, this repeat offender, I would be able to lock horns and peel his bluster like one of those prickly pears that country folk came into Seville to sell on street corners during the summer.

"Just think," I would tell him, "one turd a day, every day, in this park, for the entire length of your dog's life. As long as your dog runs free here, my kids can't, because of what they'll bring home on the bottoms of their shoes."

But when my adversary looked up from his headlong approach, he was beaming and extending his arms as if I were the priest and he the communicant.

Behold! In his unfolded hands, a sparrow chick!

"For your boys," he said. "So they can entertain themselves for a bit."

He squatted down before the wedges, holding out the baby bird so they could touch it, then gave us a quick course on how to care for it. He went so far as to pick through the nearest garbage can for something we could carry the chick home in. He found a discarded Burger King bag, pulled out a still intact Whopper box, and filled it with grass, leaves, and twigs. When the chick was snugly installed in this makeshift nest, the man said "*¡Cuídalo bien, chicos!*" (Take good care of it, boys!), and then walked off.

To me, that local character embodies what I will call "Sevillity." He might not move a muscle to spare you unpleasantness, but he'll go out of his way to give you a treat. A give and take of apathy and generosity—that's his M.O. Another way of putting it might be that he's a dove of peace capable of showering guano on your head. Thanks to him, I went instantly from seeing myself as Dirty Harry to seeing him as St. Francis of Assisi.

In general, that's how it is when casting judgments on Sevillians, or perhaps on anyone: just when you think you have them sized up, something happens to make you completely reconsider your stance.

In my adoptive city, the curtain never drops and the show can be relentless: a man shamelessly beating his dog for stopping to

sniff in a crosswalk; half a dozen school kids facing off in a free-for-all orange fight in front of a pavement café while their parents sip cocktails inside, willfully unaware; a garishly dressed, strung-out streetwalker pumping euros into a bar's slot machine, trying to wind down after the nightly grind while she's surrounded by families eating *churros* after church.

Yet the show has a flip side that's pure serendipity: two tipsy gypsies, with their guitars and tobacco-ravaged voices, converting the back of a public bus into a makeshift *tablao*; a dozen nuns, heads bent, moving like a peloton of race-walkers across Plaza de la Encarnación; a street hawker shouting as I pass with Wedge One on my shoulders, "Clean trade! Sewing machine for a green-eyed little boy!"

In short, just because people don't clean up after their dogs doesn't mean they're the shit of the city. They might even be its cream. A good way to define "Sevillity" might be when people's virtues catch you so completely off guard that their defects seem insignificant. That's about the best thing I can say about anyone.

APTO PARA NIÑOS

Perhaps the tantrum that Wedge One threw at seventeen months
on a flight from Madrid to New York was cosmic justice. He could
not fall asleep in the dry, sour, pressurized air. No doubt the six-hour
overnight drive from Seville to Madrid, done to save on airfare,
didn't help. He had spent most of it carsick. By the time we arrived
in Madrid, he was bouncing off the walls. Now, on the plane, the
pendulum had swung, and he was beside himself like I had never
seen him before, squirming, kicking, and swatting like a panicked
piglet, attracting the attention of every passenger within ten rows of
us. As I paced the airplane aisle with him, it felt like the narrowest of
all possible stages and my fellow passengers like the toughest of all
possible crowds that I had to win over with my parental talents and
skills. When, with a deft swipe, Wedge One sent my glasses whirling
into the gallery seats, I was at least spared seeing the cringing
embarrassment and scorn on my captive audience's faces after my
son's next move: kicking me in the groin, punishing the very organ
responsible for his existence.

As a last resort, I took him into the fetid, constricted
confines of the lavatory, hoping to distract him with the soap and
paper towel dispensers, or the knobs and faucet of the cereal bowl-
sized sink. Not even the thunderous suction of the cistern gave him
pause. The tantrum continued without respite, even seemed to
escalate.

I finally gave up and returned to my seat, mentally preparing
myself for six more hours of caterwauling protest. The woman in
front of us, clearly concerned that my wedge's interminable tantrum
would interrupt the restless slumber of hers, turned in her seat.

"Would you like a binky?" she asked, voice oozing with
phony commiseration.

At first I had no idea what she meant. Certain English words eluded me because I had never used them in the States. Words about baby care, for instance. To me, an infant's bodysuit was a "little frog" (*ranita*) and a breast pump a "milk extractor" (*extractor de leche*). Spanish was the language in which I had first encountered these things.

The woman held up a pacifier. Oh, that.

So as not to have to shout over my son's tantrum, I mimed spitting out the pacifier with all of his signature belligerence. Even when in the best of moods, the idea of a pacifier was anathema to him.

My compatriot recoiled. In that very moment, Wedge One also went silent, perhaps impressed by the accuracy of my imitation.

I turned to my half orange.

"Did you get a load of what she was insinuating? As if we're a couple of incompetents incapable of packing for a flight with kids."

My half orange reserved judgment at first, not trusting her English.

"She offered us a pacifier?" she asked me.

"Can you believe it?"

"A *used* pacifier?" she said.

I hadn't even thought about that.

"Exactly!" I said. "Putting on airs of moral superiority when actually she's promoting promiscuity in the most shameless of ways!"

Before I became a parent, Sevillians' patience with children would have me at wit's end. Youngsters recently released from school would claim an entire café for themselves, playing hide-and-seek or tag around tables, chairs, slot machines, cigarette dispensers, and of course me, while the mothers, somehow oblivious to the pandemonium, chattered away over *café con leche*. Afraid of throwing a tomato-faced tantrum that would make the kids' nerve-jangling racket seem like the early morning chirping of birds, I would gulp down my coffee, pack up, and head for the door, in search of a more out-of-the-way watering hole to while away the afternoon. If a cantankerous baby wound up near me, and the mother, grandmother, or nanny made no effort to mollify it, I would curse her for being remiss and the bar owner for sucking up to inconsiderate clientele.

But then the wedges were born, and everything changed. Or rather, I changed and everything else remained the same.

In Spanish, "family-friendly" has no translation, because it goes without saying. *Apto para niños* (appropriate for children) is the closest I can come up with, but that sounds like a label you might put on a film. Thanks in part to that all-American warning/welcome, I lived almost fifteen years of happy single life in the States. But ever since I became a stay-at-home dad, the idea of segregating the population according to age seems a bit frosty to me, while the idea of mixing everyone together seems outright magnanimous.

One Saturday afternoon at the local seafood joint, La Gamba Blanca (The White Prawn), there was not a seat free, or rather just one, at the very end of a group of four tables pushed together to accommodate an entire extended family. So palpable was the joy of this family celebration that Wedge One could not resist climbing out of my lap and moving over to join them. The moment he parked his diapered bottom at the head of that clan, he was welcomed with comments like, "*¡Mira quién ha llegao!*" (Look who's arrived!), "*¿Qué tal, guapetón?*" (What's up, handsome?), and "*¿Dónde te has dejado los ojos?*" (Where did you leave your eyes?)— meaning they were enormous—and then was entertained nonstop with breadsticks, key chains, and of course the furious gesticulations and explosive repartee of his hosts.

Meanwhile my half orange and I serenely finished off our seafood feast. Picking up Wedge One on our way out the door, this family that we had never seen before and would never see again gave him a hero's send-off.

"*¡A por ellos, campeón!*" (Go get 'em, champ!)

"*¡No cambies, mi alma!*" (Don't change, my soul!)

I just can't imagine anything like that ever happening in the States. That's just not how we roll. Of course, the good comes with the bad. In the States, random strangers are also less likely to tell me how to raise my kids.

When my sons and I were in the parks or playgrounds of Seville, if Wedge One wanted to climb to the top of the spidery rope tower or Wedge Two decided to shoot down some handicapped ramp while mounted on his plastic car, or if they both wanted to try the big kids' slide or to be left alone on the balance beam with no hands or to take any other reasonable—in my opinion—risk, we were likely to hear from the sidelines, "*¡Se va a caer!*" (He's going to fall!)

"Maybe," I learned to say, and then took no further precautions.

My goal was to cultivate not only initiative but curiosity in my children, although, when they were still toddlers, I'll admit that it was sometimes difficult not to precipitate the voice of alarm if I saw one of them squatting to investigate what he had stumbled upon in the street. Not to worry. "*¡Guarro! ¡Qué asco! ¡Caca!*" (Filthy! How disgusting! Poo!) would almost certainly be shouted by some passing stranger.

During the first couple of years, I suspect the meddling of the *gallinero* (henhouse) had more than a little to do with me being a man. When the wedges and I would be out doing the morning errands, women regularly bent down over the stroller to say, "*¿Dónde está mamá?*" (Where's Mommy?) When I would abandon my place in line and head for the door at the first sound of a wedge's whimpering, the *gallinero* always clucked its approval at my panicked flight, no doubt thinking I was fleeing to find *mamá*, when really I only wanted to avoid the onslaught of unsolicited advice and solve the problem on my own. More than once some well-intentioned but officious biddy had tried to lift a disgruntled wedge out of the stroller.

While the younger generations of Sevillian women claim to have evolved into the modern age and to want to share domestic and childrearing tasks with their partners, I'm not so sure.

Shortly after Wedge One was born, when my half orange and I were still in the trial-by-fire stage of parenting, we discovered that he slept an extra hour or two in the morning if we left him alone in the center of our bed after feeding him. After my wife's maternity leave ended and she was back at work, we continued with the same post-breakfast plan. One morning, when I was alone with him and thought he was dreaming milky dreams in the master bedroom, I heard what sounded like a door banging shut on our landing. It turned out to be Wedge One's head hitting the tile floor after he had fallen out of bed. Thank God it was a low bed.

When my half orange mentioned this to her friends, one of them blurted out, "How typical! The man in la-la land while the kid is left alone to fend for himself!"

This same woman, after hearing a story about a friend's toddler who shattered a glass-topped coffee table with the back of his head—also without any serious consequences, thank God—while under the care of his grandmother, piped up, "*¡Hay que tener siete ojos!*" (You have to have seven eyes!) and then shook her head in maternal solidarity.

In other words, when a woman's in charge, accidents can happen, but when a man's in charge and an accident happens, the cause is parental negligence.

One day while out for a stroll, my half orange and I bumped into a neighbor. While my wife made pleasant conversation, I kept the wedges entertained. The woman began lamenting the fact that her daughter, who also had small children, sometimes worked late and therefore had to go to desperate lengths to find someone to pick them up at daycare. She made an airy gesture toward me and said to my wife, "Since you've got the nanny at home..."

"Nanny, your sister's *coño*!" I almost said.

My half orange tells me that I take things too much to heart. Perhaps I do relish playing the victim. Perhaps Sevillian women aren't as sexist as they seem. My half orange isn't sexist, not really. One Saturday morning, she called to ask what fruit and vegetables we needed. After giving her the list, I heard her explain to the greengrocer that normally she had a look in the kitchen before stepping out, but with two kids in diapers, and her husband caught up in his work, blah, blah, blah...

"I couldn't have him thinking that you ran the household," she told me later.

God knows I don't. I've just become *apto para niños*, and therefore more *apto* in general.

MORE THAN A WORLD APART

Wedge One could walk and almost run at nine months, while Wedge Two could not even turn over in his crib at that age. When we would sit him up, he would tip over and lay sprawled exactly as gravity had left him until someone set him upright again. When he finally got the hang of moving on his own, it happened so quickly that my half orange and I wondered if he had been toying with us all along, perhaps to draw attention away from his brother. A month and a half later, he could stand up and walk, sometimes with such determination and impulse that he would catch Wedge One off guard, wrenching away whatever had provoked his hurtling pursuit.

My wedges see the world as differently as they move in it. When I first started pointing things out to Wedge One, he'd study the tip of my finger with consummate interest, and what he discovered there never seemed to disappoint him. When Wedge Two was about the same age, he would turn his gaze instantly and instinctively to where I pointed, like one of those Iberian lynxes.

As they've grown, Wedge Two's vision remains more outward, incisive, and hungry, while Wedge One is more analytical, thorough, and patient. Physically, Wedge One's agility continues to stand out, but Wedge Two often trumps it with resolve.

My older son has skin the color of Mojave sandstone, greenish-blue eyes, and curly, golden-brown hair. The younger one's complexion is milky white, his hair chestnut brown, and his eyes black beneath the shadow of his long, thick lashes. I praise God for each unique set of features, but what strikes me as a blessing beyond compare is the equally robust health and life that shines forth from both of them.

Wedge One is noble and refined. Once, when he was three and playing in Amate Park's pea gravel with a younger boy, a kid came along and yanked the plastic shovel out of his playmate's hand.

Wedge One yanked it back and returned it to its owner. The bully about-faced and walked off. Order restored.

Wedge Two can be rough. He once stood astride his balance bike, refusing to let go, as another kid grabbed onto the handlebars and tried to take it away. The kid bent down to bite him on the arm. Wedge Two watched coolly, withstanding the pain, and with his free arm began pummeling the kid's back with elbows, bringing him to his knees.

"*¡Guerreros!*" (Warriors!) said the other boy's father, rushing forward to separate them.

It was Wedge Two's audacity that ended up capturing the attention of Luz Marina, the Paraguayan girl next door. His self-possession when laying claim to whatever she brought to the playground made her wary around him, mostly in vain. If her guard dropped for an instant, Wedge Two would snatch the coveted item away, with Luz Marina's parents insisting that she learn to share. Meanwhile, Wedge One, as angelic in nature as in countenance, would try hopelessly to cheer her up with corn puffs. So it went, day after day. Wedge Two would incite her wrath and Wedge One would feel it, because Luz Marina took her tantrums out on whichever wedge was within range.

Wedge Two's birth was more spectacular than his brother's. In Spanish public hospitals, if complications arise in the delivery room, fathers must leave. Wedge One pushed and pushed at the birth canal but refused to commit. This, coincidentally or not, would turn out to be telling of his character—easily distracted, often enjoying the journey so much that he forgets about the destination. The doctors finally decided on forceps, so I had to step out. I only *heard* him emerge into the world as I stood in a dark hallway at 4 a.m., staring at the stripe of light shining through the delivery room's swinging doors. When the nurses called me back in and handed him over, he went suddenly silent in my arms, staring up wide-eyed, listening to me talk. I don't recall what I said, only my certainty that he understood.

The birth of Wedge Two happened so fast it nearly caught me looking the other way. The nurse who received us on the birthing ward got one look at my wife, literally staggering, and said, "*¿Qué quieres, chiquilla, un cubata o una cervecita?*" (What can I get you, kiddo, a rum and Coke or a brew?) Wedge Two shot into the world as if out of a flume, chin bent to his chest, shoulders up against his ears, and arms pressed flat to his sides, not even giving the doctors time to inject his mother with the epidural. He, too, went quiet in my arms, but, if births are a prelude of things to come, then perhaps his serenity was tinged with the self-satisfaction of having taken us all aback, for having given us a good but gratuitous scare.

In my formative years, I got to know New York fully but without urgency, like a child who learns what the world is like by putting it piece by piece into his mouth. I got to know Seville much later, cautiously but with longing, like a proud but timid Romeo, waiting for the object of his desires to declare herself first. Until I got a weekly column in the local paper—and felt appreciated, even esteemed—I never tried to explain the love I felt for a city or for family, despite these being the very things that had formed and defined me.

The first time I spent a week away from the wedges, I was greeted on my return by Wedge One hiding his face in my half orange's chest, perhaps overwhelmed by his feelings for me. A gust of wind once blew him down on a Cádiz beach; I watched him get back to his feet on his own. Wedge Two's highchair once tipped forward and crashed to the floor with him still in it, but he crawled away unharmed and unfazed. When I tripped and fell in the park one day, Wedge One stood perplexed and at a loss, while Wedge Two rushed over to grip and pull with all his might the hand I held out to him.

They rekindle my capacity for wonder every day.

I hope as my wedges grow up, they come to understand that, although their mother and I are no longer in top form or perhaps even present, that only adds to our story and therefore augments us. We are who we are, and who we once were, simultaneously. I want

to be for my wedges what they are for me, like the two cities I call home, but more so. Something to measure significance by—what's temporary and what's permanent, what's fleeting and what's eternal. The more we miss each other, the more we feel each other's presence; the more we feel each other's presence, the more we're reminded of who we've been and what we might become.

The first time I walked the streets of Seville, pierced by an arrow, marveling at what I saw, I felt as though New York had prepared me for it. I felt oddly at home. Years later, when Seville really was my home, an old man, accompanied by his caretaker, stopped in his tracks, choked up, and called out to my boys, "*¡Os quiero!*" (I love you!) His outburst did not seem strange to me. I knew about love at first sight and how deep it can run, trailing clouds of glory from other great loves.

The Spanish like to say, "*Cada niño es un mundo aparte*" (Every child is a world apart), the implication being that we should not compare them. The writer Evelyn Waugh once said, "Comparisons are odious." Well, I compare my sons for the same reason that I compare cities, languages, and cultures—so that they become more distinct and clear, to help me define what love and home are, to help anchor me in place, so that nothing can be erased. Because if I ever lost any of this, my world would come apart.

SWEET SOMETHINGS

WARRING STEREOTYPES

If you could only see the intricate contraptions that I fabricated to hide the three dust-clogged air conditioners that protruded from the walls of my half orange's two-bedroom apartment in Madre de Dios. The eyesores had been there when she bought the place; who knows how long they'd been kaput. Because removing them would have required masons, plasterers, and painters to cover up the gaping holes in our walls, I decided to volunteer for a task of home improvement. To assure that the final product met my impossibly high standards, the job took me, without exaggeration, three eight-hour shifts, with occasional breaks to keep my eyes from becoming permanently crossed. We were still in the honeymoon phase back then. It's possible that my snugly-fitting encasements finally convinced her that I was a man with whom she could start a family. All of her friends, upon seeing my handiwork, would gasp with admiration and amazement. Each box was unique, one-of-a-kind, the work of an artist possessed.

Despite the happy result, the project killed once and for all my gumption for DIY home improvements. Actually, no. At my half orange's instigation, I also lined our bedroom closet and its diabolically dimensioned shelves with decorative paper: two interminable days of measuring, cutting, and pasting to make sure that even its most hidden corners did not end up exposed. That was absolutely the last straw. After that, the closest thing to DIY that I agreed to undertake was to construct the most elemental IKEA furniture, and I did this only on the nonnegotiable condition that my wife and kids left me completely alone in the house until the job was done. That way I could curse and punch doors when I discovered that IKEA's designers, upon producing idiot-proof assembly instructions, had not accounted for consumers quite as idiotic as me.

My half orange does not go to such extremes. If she mends a hole in the pocket of my jeans, it's possible that the hole will reopen the next time I wear them. She just shrugs it off and sews it up again when she gets the chance. If at the supermarket she fails to find all that she's looking for, she doesn't do what I do, which is head off in a black cloud of frustration and self-sacrifice to another supermarket in order to return home in spiteful triumph with everything that was on the list. She goes back another day—or not, settling instead for eating some hodgepodge meal that week or perhaps ordering a pizza.

Sevillians tend to typecast *estadounidenses* as overwrought and neurotic in how we keep on top of things, while the general take on Andalusians is that they settle for whatever, as long as it works. In other words, my wife and I represent warring cultural stereotypes, and our relationship their eternal battleground (or at least the frequently disputed border).

My wife claims that I am incapable of doing two things at once. I counter that I cannot do two things *well* at once, so if I do mistakenly attempt to multitask, I quickly leave one task to finish later, in order to have the pleasure of at least one job well done.

My wife is always finding my shoes, backpack, or even bags of groceries abandoned in the middle of the living room, or the butt end of the TV remote emerging from the top of the fridge, or my lost book at the bottom of the playpen exactly where I left it. Just before leaving for work, I am always in desperate search of my keys, wallet, or glasses, or sometimes all three at once, asking her in ever more accusing tones if she has happened to see them.

My excuse is that whatever distracted me from the other balls in the air, whether it was the outstretched arms of an attention-seeking wedge, an idea for an article, or the last few minutes of a ball game, I devoted my full attention to it, and my objective was wholly and satisfactorily met.

With my half orange, on the other hand, regardless if she is doing various things at once or focusing on a single task, regardless if she is distracted or interrupted or if the wedges are sound asleep

or bouncing off the walls, the result is always the same: it lacks follow-through.

If she washes the dishes, she puts them in the drying rack in such a way that when I store them in the cupboard later, water sluices off and wets my clothes to the skin. If she cooks spaghetti, she leaves it hot in the strainer and it cools into a solid mass of loops and tangles resembling brains, which then has to be cut into pieces if anyone is hungry enough to eat it. When she takes out the garbage, she doesn't replace the bag, so if I end up dumping some plate of slop without looking first—an oversight that a just world would not punish me for—I have to scoop it out again and wipe the sides clean before lining the pail as my wife should have done.

Her excuse, quite reasonable, is that, at the end of the day, none of what I bitch about really matters, and furthermore, the struggle to achieve perfection in life's daily and interminable domestic tasks is exhausting and contrary to peace and happiness.

Of course, I know many Andalusians who not only resist the stereotype that my wife sometimes embodies but would be offended at the mere suggestion of it. Perhaps they are as torn up inside by petty obsessions and inflated self-opinion as I am. I would prefer to be my wife any day of the week, as long as I don't have to catch a train, do the family finances, or read the fine print on a contract. She not only enjoys life more than I do, she also understands it better. She accepts its conditions, rather than trying to change them so that they meet some unnatural, egoistic demand. When I criticize my half orange for being lazy and apathetic, it's envy speaking, pure and simple.

When my parents left New York and found the ideal plot of land at the base of Kearsarge Mountain in the backwoods of New Hampshire, my mother set out to build her dream house. A boss once evaluated her as "meticulously precise," and everyone in our family agrees that never has a redundancy been so properly employed. During the construction of the house, she kept relentlessly on top of the contractors so that the finished product would be exactly as she had so fastidiously imagined it. When the work was done, anyone but the single-minded, ruthlessly striving type that my dear mother is would have considered it a dream come true. But to her, the posts of the wooden rail on the back porch were not symmetrically distributed. And she's right; they're not. Since she pointed this out to me, I cannot help seeing this lack of symmetry rather than the unsymmetrical majesty of Mount Kearsarge, which the porch was built to tranquilly observe.

If my mother lived with us in Seville, she would attempt to bring our place up to snuff, hiring workers to do what she could not do herself. Either they would walk off the job in protest at her tireless demands or she would suffer an attack of shingles for being so nonchalantly thwarted by them. And all the while, I would be racing around the apartment, cursing under my breath as I searched for my keys, wallet, or glasses, and my blessed half orange would be sewing the pocket of my jeans for the umpteenth time, the only one in a good mood.

If I had to sum up our relationship with two Spanish expressions, I'd choose *matar moscas con cañonazos* (to kill flies with cannon blasts) and *¡Que me quiten lo bailao!* (Let's see them take away the already-danced!)

The first is the Spanish version of "to make a mountain out of a molehill." Killing flies with cannon blasts is how I try to solve minor problems when at my worst—with unnecessary firepower that ends up doing lots of collateral damage.

Meanwhile, "*¡Que me quiten lo bailao!*" is what Andalusians say when they have lived it up at the expense of more pressing concerns. Now, as the pressing concerns come to bear, the revelers recall "the already-danced" as consolation. George Gershwin wrote "They Can't Take That Away from Me" to capture the feeling. Also, there's the expression "We'll always have Paris!" But for me "the already-danced" nails it best. My half orange has led me into dances—true love, family life, complete cultural immersion—that I would never have danced had I stubbornly stuck to my plans.

PEACE AND TRANQUILITY ON THE BEACH

My half orange and I were sitting on the beach in Ogunquit, Maine, on a gorgeous July day, but only Wedge One, eighteen months old and naked except for his diaper, was truly enjoying the water, sun, and sand.

My wife, having lived her entire life where temperatures can reach 120 degrees, just a hop, skip, and a jump from beautiful beaches on both the Atlantic and Mediterranean coasts, looked on high at the brilliant sun, then down at the dark one-piece she was wearing.

"*Me siento muy moro,*" (I feel quite Moorish,) she said.

Not a bikini or thong in sight, and the only topless females were under the age of five.

"As you can see," I said, "you fit in quite well."

"What's wrong with these people?" she said. "Are they in mourning?"

Back home, my half orange walks around our apartment dressed like one of Charlie's Angels. When she comes home from work and says, "I'm going to get comfortable," that means that if someone knocks at the door, I have to answer it if we don't want to kick up a scandal on the landing. Before our trip to the States, I had warned her that she was going to have to be more discreet with her wardrobe while we stayed with my folks. That was why, for the first time in her life, she was sitting on the beach wearing clothes that concealed more than they revealed.

"It's a good thing we forgot your bikini back home," I said. "Or rather, those three eye-patches strung together that the manufacturer had the audacity to call clothing. The locals would have called the police."

"What a dreary country!"

"A bit starchy, yes, depending on where you live. But I think 'proper' might be the better word. You Andalusian women have no mercy. Only a man with herculean mental focus can enjoy building a sand castle with his sons if twenty yards away two college girls are playing beach paddle with their bare brown titties bouncing around more than the ball."

"Bare, brown, and bouncing like balls, huh? From twenty yards away you can see all that? And you say you need glasses to drive! Well, let me tell you something, when I see a young stud, you think I don't perk up? Why do you think we mothers go to firefighter exhibitions with our sons?"

"All I'm trying to say, love, is that Mérimée set *Carmen* in Seville for a reason. Sex appeal can incite men to murder, and that's no joke, which is why I believe women like you should go to the beach well-covered, at least in places like this or in Chipiona, which attract a family crowd."

"The beach in Chipiona is full of Sevillian fishwives eating *salchichón* sandwiches and watermelon!"

"The last time we were there, I spent the entire day looking down at the sand. You women paraded your boobs around like crown jewels. Not the slightest respect for the tragic male weakness."

"What is it about your culture that causes forty-year-old men to fall to pieces like pimply teenagers before a topless woman on the beach?"

"If Spanish men don't complain about the boobfest, that's because they're masochists. Personally, I go to the beach to participate in *wholesome* fun. Why would women from your tribe, supposedly so given over to the institution of family, want to deprive me of this? Just because a man has a wife and kids doesn't mean his blood's stopped flowing."

"Right. Through the main vein."

"Fine, take potshots. Turn sex into a joke. But just so you know, that day in Chipiona, I swore I would never again fake sophistication or pretend indifference. The next time I saw bare boobs on the beach, I was going to pick up my stuff and find a different place to sit."

"Next to bigger, bouncier, browner boobs."

"Laugh all you want. Just don't be surprised if you show your boobs in public and perverts start recording videos."

"Now I understand why Janet Jackson's nipple caused such an uproar here, and why your president got raked over the coals for having an affair with his secretary."

"It wasn't Janet Jackson's nipple that offended us; it was how she used it to call attention to herself. As far as Bill Clinton, he wasn't caught with his secretary but with an intern. Our elected president was willing to risk the dignity of his job, his country, and his wife, and therefore his credibility and effectiveness, just so he could get off with some political groupie in the Oval Office—the same place where Abraham Lincoln freed the slaves."

"Maybe he was trying to free the country of a different kind of ball and chain."

"Well, I want that ball and chain," I said. "It helps keep me in check."

"I don't know what to tell you. Pray the rosary on the beach to enjoy yourself."

"I don't need to here. That's the whole point."

"Well, I can't enjoy the beach wearing so many clothes."

"A small sacrifice for a good cause: male peace of mind."

"Well, on Andalusian beaches you're sacrificing for a good cause, too: women's social freedoms."

I let her have the last word, so I could finally enjoy just the sun, the sand, and the sea.

SPANISH FRENCH TOAST

My half orange and I had travelled to the town of Écija to see a bullfight, only to find the *plaza* (ring) shut up without a soul in sight twenty minutes before the scheduled start time. Turned out that the local *torero* (bullfighter) had broken with his manager over money, and the event had been cancelled. The barman in the *torero*'s fan club returned our money without objection, peeling it off a fat roll of bills.

"*Así es la vida cuando no eres figurón,*" (Such is life when you're not a big name,) he said and shrugged.

True enough, except my half orange and I had been looking forward to the show. At least I had been.

We meandered back to the town's main drag and sat down at a terraced café for some coffee. Holy Week was coming up, so my half orange ordered *torrijas*, a kind of cold French toast soaked in honey. We ate and people-watched, a pale substitute for the spectacle we had come for. I wondered if maybe we could reenact our own version of time-honored forces pitted against each other. Finally I spotted someone I could use as a cape.

"Get a load of buff boy over there," I said, "shrink-wrapped in designer clothes, peacocking at the head of the family parade. And there's his dumpy wife lagging behind, pushing the double stroller and pulling another kid by the hand."

"Maybe he works some sports-related job," said my wife, hardly looking, "or at a clothes shop, where he gets a discount. Could be a firefighter, I guess."

"In his dreams," I said. "He's a wannabe Don Juan who vents his frustrations while cultivating false illusions of sexual prowess by spending two hours a day in the gym."

That got her attention.

"What do you know?" she said. "Maybe too much."

"Hey," I said. "I'm not the one who goes three nights a week to the municipal pool."

She put down her fork with a clink against the plate.

"I swim, darling, so that I don't turn into the dumpy wife, burdened by children, trailing behind the rooster. One day, looking in the mirror, I asked you, 'Do you think my butt is getting bigger?' Do you remember your response?"

"Nope."

"Silence."

"You should be grateful I don't lie to you!" I said. "Tough guy over there with his Ray-Bans and sideburns and his inflatable physique lacks the *casta* and *cojones* to tell his half orange the truth."

She sighed and picked up her fork again.

"The poor thing probably doesn't have time to go to the gym."

"She has time to eat," I replied.

"*¡Coño!*" My gorgeous *toro* finally charged. "Let the woman eat what she wants!" She stabbed what remained of *torrija* and polished it off with fury. "We wives don't sleep, don't screw, don't leave the house, and now we're not allowed to eat? Might as well just blow our brains out!"

"Simmer down, *cariño*. It's nothing personal," I said.

"Nothing personal, he says!"

"Hey, I like your spare tires. More to snuggle up to in bed."

"*¡Y una porra!*" (And a nightstick!)

"More for that to snuggle up to, too," I said.

I imagined the crowd on its feet, chanting, "*¡To-re-ro! ¡To-re-ro!*" (Bull-fight-er! Bull-fight-er!), the band striking up a *paso doble*. Time for the *matador* to take command, showing poise, panache, and deft cape work.

"A woman's sexual appetite," I began, "is generally driven by a wider range of factors than a man's."

"In your dreams!"

"And different ones."

"If thinking that consoles you…"

"The average woman can make love to her man to encourage him, to please him, or even to pity him, and still manage to enjoy herself."

"Right, with her eyes shut, imagining the gas man above her."

"And so, if that musclebound metrosexual and his kind really want to find satisfaction in their sexual lives, they need to look for it *inside* their marriages, which, by definition, are rooted in tolerance, acceptance, and forgiveness."

"Is that from the catechism?"

"C'mon," I said. "How many times have we talked about the type of Sevillian skirt chaser seen prowling cocktail lounges at three in the morning and then seen again on Sunday in the town center, taking a morning stroll with his childhood sweetheart, now wife, and their dolled up progeny? Seville isn't like New York, where you can hide your philandering. Here, your spouse might be the last to know, but everybody else is hip to your game. Cheaters don't just cheat in Seville; they expose their entire families to ridicule. But only the most shameless pricks do it. The city saves the rest of us."

"So if we lived in New York, you'd be getting some on the side?"

"I'm saying that your city teaches the average, well-meaning guy where his happiness lies—with his juicy gem of a wife."

The brilliance of my *toreo* could not be denied. With mastery and a cool hand, I had made us dance as one.

Still mesmerized, eyes fixed on the beyond, my half orange said something under her breath.

One had to be careful. She was always a threat.

"What?" I said, leaning forward.

"My happiness," she said, "lies in eating whatever I *coño* feel like."

She headed to the counter for more Spanish French toast, having tossed me like a ragdoll to the sand.

Torrijas trumped *toreros* in Écija that afternoon.

CHRISTMAS HEAT

My London friend K, a psychoanalyst, had introduced me to the self-help book *The Way of the Superior Man* by David Deida. K's former girlfriend, a yoga instructor, had recommended it to him. So impressed was he by the content and by the woman's aura and apparent insight into men that he decided to have a child with her. Six months after the child was born, the couple split up, and then continued to bicker in separation.

Despite the broken and quarrelsome set of parents that the book had helped beget, I thought Deida was on to something with his main idea—that love was feminine and freedom masculine, and that the proportion of feminine and masculine in each of us dictated the extent to which we lived for love and/or freedom.

I bought the book in Spanish for my half orange, but when I presented it to her, she scoffed.

"That's a cliché," she said.

"No," I said. "The cliché is that women live for love and men for freedom. Deida is pointing out that there are masculine and feminine sides to all of us."

"And the feminine side of the 'superior man,' is that what makes him superior?" she said, which ended the conversation.

Still, I could not help thinking that deep down, whether she realized it or not, she and Deida coincided in their thinking, and that she epitomized his idea of the feminine.

Perhaps it's a cultural thing—her being Sevillian, Andalusian, Latin, Old World, or a combination of all the above—that gives her no qualms about reining me in. Talking to ex-girlfriends, for instance, is prohibited. "What do you have to say to them that you can't say to me?" she says. Fair enough, but the issue goes deeper. Although guys like me believe we have voluntarily retired from the game, she feels that we continue to have the latent desire to play it, so she takes precautions, perhaps for my own benefit. She never lets me forget that, no matter how committed I think I am to her, I could easily slip up.

"Remember, you only sleep the siesta with me," she'll say, seeing me off to work when I have a one-on-one intensive class with a beautiful woman.

Once while visiting the States, I got invited to New York to give a talk at the Instituto Cervantes. The fact that I was going to be back the same day did not quiet her fears.

"Who will you see?" she asked.

"Nobody," I said, but she was not reassured.

"What would you do if I were a travelling salesman?" I asked.

"Travel with you," she said.

She has absolutely no patience for people whose theories on romantic relationships flaunt what she calls "*las cosas como son*" (things as they are).

Once, she came home from work stewing over what a colleague had told her.

"Charo tells me that whenever she's out with her husband and they see a beautiful woman, she insists that he look at her, egging him on with comments like, 'Sexy, right?' or 'What a great body!' She says if she doesn't 'openly share' with him the 'natural desire' to 'admire' these women, he'll start fantasizing. Have you ever heard a dumber idea? Men don't admire gorgeous women; they want to take them to bed."

According to my Sevillian friend Victor, another aspiring "superior man," this tendency in Andalusian women to keep their men on a short leash should be piqued on occasion. One night, after I had dragged him for *tapas* after class and the evening ended late, he turned on his mobile phone and saw twenty-two missed calls from his fiancée.

"Did I get you in trouble?" I said.

"Are you kidding?" he replied. "This is good for the relationship! Women can never forget that we're men and we're alive."

All this was running through my mind the night my half orange and I were invited, wedges included, to a dinner party one Christmas Eve in the States.

At first I had liked that the tables were turned. For once, she was the exotic one and I was simply the exotic one's companion. Our hosts' home in Wilmot, New Hampshire, had once been the house of a mink farmer, and before that a roadside inn. That night its antique and rural charm was accompanied by every imaginable festive touch: an authentic and aromatic spruce in the living room, the branches decorated with starry lights and rustic handmade ornaments. Presents stood piled at the foot of it. A fire crackled in the hearth. One of the hosts' daughters sang Christmas carols, while the other played a grand piano, its lid lit with cinnamon-scented candles.

I was pleased to see my half orange experiencing a *Navidad estadounidense* to its dreamy Rockwellian extremes, pleased to finally be just a member of the supporting cast, until I realized that my humble role meant that while she rubbed shoulders and received the royal treatment, I had to run behind the wedges, making sure they did not tumble the tree, throw holiday knickknacks into the fire, or quench their thirst with sips of abandoned Chardonnay.

Still, I bore with it to the end, smiling through my growing ill-humor. Just as we were getting ready to leave, I got my chance to shine when the other darling of the evening, a local long-haired tech millionaire who had retired at forty-five to buy, restore, and resell beautifully situated homes like the one we were in, cornered me near the coat rack and asked, with far too much intensity, "Is it true that the Spanish are a sensuous people?"

I paused to give the question serious thought, then replied, "My wife is Andalusian more than Spanish. As far as being, as you say, sensuous, let's just say she's capable of missing a plane if she's soaking in a hot bath."

Mr. Moneybags, instead of beaming at my attempt at wit, gave a forced and insipid smile.

On the drive home, still cringing at the interaction, I tried to get my wife to confirm his poor sense of humor. Instead she said, clearly tickled, "He was eating me with his eyes all evening."

"Son of a bitch!" I said. "Of course! Now his response makes sense—the grin of a masochist after being kicked in the balls. Well, I'm glad, *glad* to have destroyed the blessed tranquility of his Christmas."

She looked at me like I was insane.

"Keep your voice down," she whispered. "The children."

"The children, says the starlet of the soirée! The children, honey, are sound asleep in back, exhausted after doing a half million laps around the plantation manor, with me tagging behind. But you didn't notice that, did you? No, not Cleopatra, sprawled on the divan, playing court to her admirers."

"What are you implying?"

"Andalusian women should come with a warning, like cigarettes!"

"How many glasses of wine did you drink?"

"Couldn't be soberer, actually. Thank God I met you when you were almost forty and had learned not to abuse your power too much. Thank God I had already lived in Seville for a year and was steeled against the onslaught of sexual insinuation—"

"I insinuated nothing at all with that man!"

"You didn't have to! It's unconscious! That's what makes you dangerous! Especially with that poor bastard, surrounded by snow for seven months a year. He absolutely did *not* see the Sevillian Christmas nymph coming."

"So now I'm a nymph?"

"I'm not blaming you! *Las cosas como son.*"

She turned away, staring out the window at the snowy, mountainous landscape, illuminated by moonlight.

"I can't be the only guy," I said, "who, walking the streets of Seville, curses the heavens for being born a man. Was it Luis

Buñuel who said he didn't find happiness till he got old enough to lose his libido? If he'd lived in Seville, he'd have been masturbating too much to make films."

That got a rise out of her.

"*¡Los cojones te ato!* (I tie up your balls!) Take a pill!"

"What pill is that?"

"The one they give to soldiers on missions so they don't get horny!"

"Why don't I get offers for that in my spam folder?"

Outside the car a cold snap had set in, but inside, with the heater going full blast and so many layers of clothes and passion, we were incubating Sevillian summer.

"No wonder in ancient times they locked you up in fortress-like homes, barred the windows, and policed you with eunuchs," I said.

She stared at me, eyes twinkling, then burst out laughing. She leaned over and planted a kiss on my temple.

"More later," she added. "I don't want you getting distracted at the wheel."

Just like that, our spat was settled.

Love and freedom: my half orange embodies both. Every ounce of my "superior woman" is uncategorizable.

ANNIHILATED

When my half orange finally emerged half-asleep from the bedroom on her way to the kitchen to make breakfast, it was 9:30 a.m.—exactly the time that she and her sister had agreed to meet in a café to discuss family matters. I had already been awake for an hour, counting the minutes.

I've spent my entire life fighting the clock. When I got married, I thought I would gain an ally in this futile crusade. Fat chance. My wife fails to feel my pain. Well, she would feel it this morning, because my nemesis was sneaking up on her from behind, fangs bared, ready to pounce. I would watch gloatingly as she woke with a start from her fog of sleep, remembering her now-missed appointment with her sister, her poor sister, although she had probably slept through the rendezvous too.

Out of the corner of my eye, I watched my wife idly prepare her coffee and toast and then settle down across from me with an enormous yawn.

"Aren't you working?" she asked when the yawn finally released its hold on her.

I did not look up from the book open before me.

"I'm reading. A very instructive book. *The Shadow of the Sun*, by Ryszard Kapuściński. It's teaching me, for example, that I'm married to an African."

"Who? Me?"

"You're not European, that's for sure."

She took a bite of her toast and chewed pensively.

"For my sense of musical rhythm?"

"The only rhythm that doesn't exist for you, *cariño*, is tick-tock tick-tock."

"You'll excuse me if I don't understand your irony at this hour of the morning."

"At this hour of the morning? And what hour do you think that is?"

"Kiddo, considering that it's Saturday, you appear a bit tense."

"You know very well that if I wake up at the same time as the boys, I spend the entire morning trying in vain to get out of the hole that I've got myself in. Waking up at the crack of dawn is one of the many sacrifices I make to be an organized parent."

"Are you saying I'm not an organized parent?"

"I'm saying that you're a Nubian queen. Time stops for you."

"I'm not your slave, that's true."

"I should have known what to expect since that day I overheard you reminiscing about missing the bus to Murcia on your way to Ibiza because you were eating an enormous breakfast in the train station and were caught up in conversation with your partner in crime, what's her name, the Brazilian, another Nubian queen…"

"Celia. We *almost* missed it. Twice! First in Seville and again in Granada, the second time because we were eating lunch. What a pair of turkeys we are!" She laughed in retrospect.

"Sure," I said. "What a riot. But the bus doesn't wait for anyone, not even two Nubian queens. Schedules exist for a reason."

"Right, but I don't think about that when I'm on vacation."

"Of course not. You're thinking about the sandwich you're eating. Listen to this and tell me if you can relate." I opened Kapuściński's book and began to read aloud. "'For Africans, time is a loose category, open, elastic and subjective… it disappears if we ignore it or stop imposing ourselves on it… it retreats into a state of hibernation, or even to nothingness, if we don't lend it our energy.'"

"I am in complete and absolute agreement with that statement," said my half orange.

"Yes," I said. "Time disappears. And so does the bus. I suppose that your empathy with the Africans is a result of your culture having lived for eight hundred years under Moorish rule."

"Al-Ándalus, not Moorish."

"Yeah, yeah. You just go with the flow. Always. Well, I'll tell you where that leads you 95 percent of the time: nowhere."

"Unlike you, I don't live in mortal fear that I'm not going to get where I want to go. For me, my vacation starts the moment I catch the bus."

"Or don't catch it."

"Hey, we caught it and we got to our destination. We Andalusians always get where we want to. Although it might not seem like it to you, we've got the situation under control. Relax, honey. You'll get where you want just the same."

"Have you noticed that every time we're going somewhere as a family, I'm the one who has to keep an eye on the clock, or we might never even leave the house at all?"

"If the neurotic I'm married to is going to worry eighty thousand times more than necessary, why am I going to worry, too? And on top of that suffer the effects of your constipation for however long it takes to get there?"

I could not have laid the trap better. She was right where I wanted her. I leaned back in my chair and stretched.

"By the way, honey, what time is it?"

"It's Saturday morning. Time doesn't exist."

"Well, the neurotic *estadounidense* says that yes, time exists." I looked at my watch. "It is…fifteen minutes past when you were supposed to have met up with your sister."

"What are you talking about?"

"Your appointment with your sister this morning at 9:30."

"Oh, we put that off."

"Put it off? But…well… Oh, sure! Always put off till tomorrow what you can do today. The motto of the Nubian queen."

She ignored me to grab Kapuściński's book and pick up where I had left off.

"'The European depends on and answers to time… In order to exist and function, all its ironclad and inexorable laws must be observed… deadlines, dates, days and hours must be respected…

Between man and time an unresolvable conflict is created, a conflict that always ends with man losing: time annihilates him.'"

"Nobody tells me anything in this house," I said.

"Maybe the clock was ticking too loudly for you to hear," she said.

GUTTER TALK

There is a phrase in Spanish—*¡Mucha mierda!* (Lots of shit!)— used like "Knock 'em dead!" in English. The idiom goes back to a time when lots of horse shit in the streets after a theatrical performance meant that the public was flocking to see it. I have always hesitated to use the phrase, owing to its touch of Sevillian *guasa* (snideness)—as though it wished well with an undercut.

I did, however, say it to myself every Friday when my half orange and I would leave the wedges at my sister-in-law's and stroll a few blocks to Bar Enrique on Calle Arroyo (Gutter Street) to spend some quality time together.

On one of those Fridays, still early, I was actually able to make it to the bar and get served. At a packed bar in Seville, either my half orange orders or we head somewhere else.

That morning I had received two surprising pieces of news. First, my sister, who a few years earlier had left journalism to become a schoolteacher in order to spend more time with her kids, had now cut completely loose from the professional world to be a full-time stay-at-home mom. And second, the wife of a friend of mine had left her top management position in a bank to focus entirely on parenting as well. The fact that both of these women had accomplished more in their careers and earned higher salaries than their husbands had not deterred them. It seemed to me that a kind of social reactionism was afoot in my country, still inconceivable in recently modernized Spain. I wondered if my half orange was aware of all this.

I returned to our table with two ice-cold Cruzcampos, ordering duties flawlessly fulfilled, ready to put her to the test. We would see just how alternative she really was. As usual, I would need *mucha mano izquierda* (a lot of left hand), a bullfighting metaphor meaning "finesse."

"One of the first times you impressed me was in this bar," I began. "We'd hardly been going out two months and you brought me here. The mob extended out to the sidewalk terrace. You left me on the fringes to go order. I watched you raise a hand to part the crowd, which then swallowed you up. Minutes passed. It seemed like hours. I had the absurd notion that you weren't coming back. I wondered, *Should I just go home?* Then suddenly an eerie silence descended and your tiny voice exploded out, ordering adamantly. If I'd gone to order, I'd still be waiting six years later for the barman to acknowledge my existence. In that moment I knew I could not live without you, in Seville or anywhere else." I raised my beer in tribute. "Cheers to my Sevillian savior."

"How romantic," she said. "How many of your articles do I have to edit today?"

"None. Today we just chat. Time for a heart-to-heart, my love. I want to get to the bottom of you."

"Careful. I might just surprise you."

"Wouldn't want it any other way." I settled in for some fun. "Without further ado," I began, "would you consider yourself a feminist?"

"I consider myself a woman."

I leaned over and planted a kiss on her lips.

"That's why I'm more in love with you every day," I said. "Tell me, if you don't mind, the most agreeable moment of your day."

She did not have to give the question much thought.

"Without a doubt, when I wake up, eat breakfast alone, savor my toast and coffee, then take a shower, put on powders and cream, get dressed up, put on perfume—"

"What about spending time with your children?!" I said.

"You asked for the most agreeable moment of my day, not the best. And you haven't let me finish. After this very pleasant ritual in which I'm taking care of only myself, I get to the office and am hit smack in the face with reality."

"Now we're getting somewhere. And the worst moment of your day?"

"The last hour of work always seems endless, as does the hour just before you get home from teaching at night, when I'm tired from being alone with the kids all afternoon."

"Okay, let's focus on the first moment. As a mother of small children, do you find office work fulfilling?"

"Well, it's a physical rest, because I'm seated the whole time, but it's psychologically draining, because I can't disconnect from the boys. You men are able to disconnect. When you're working, you're working. When you're watching sports, you're watching sports. When you're with friends, you're 100 percent with friends. Women don't work that way, or at least I don't. But the worst is the powerlessness I feel when I can't take my kids to the doctor when they're sick, or be at home caring for them, or go with them to school on special days. The feminists talk about freedom. I don't know how working women are more free, except perhaps economically, or that they've earned the right to demand that their husbands do more housework."

"In the supposed case that my salary was large enough to support the family, would you stop working?"

"I doubt you're ready for that."

"I'm sure that with time I could find a full-time job that fits my talents and tastes."

"That's not what I mean. I'm talking about what I would need from you if I dedicated all my time to the house and children. I would wait with even more expectation for you to return from work, because I wouldn't have talked to another adult all day."

"I think I would rise to the occasion."

"That's what you say now. Charo's husband, when he went back to work after spending five days alone with the kids, said to her, 'Even if I'm unloading trucks, I couldn't be happier.' Two weeks later, this same guy arrived home from work, saw the TV on, and accused Charo of sitting on her ass all afternoon watching gossip shows."

"Not all men are the same, hon. My country isn't perfect, but men take women a little less for granted."

She shook her head.

"When the woman is at home, sooner or later she ends up having to do everything."

"Okay, I agree that we men have to fight the temptation to slack off on housework, but don't you prefer being at home to being at work? Don't you feel like it's more important? Tedious at times, like anything, but more fulfilling at the end of the day?"

"To be fulfilled, I need to be appreciated."

"But I appreciate you!"

"I want to keep it that way."

"How could that ever change?" I looked towards the bar, which was starting to fill. "We should probably order food, hon. People are waiting for tables."

"Go ahead, big guy. I'll wait here demurely for your return."

"You know how I am with crowds…"

She stood with a sigh.

"One more thing, and we'll drop the subject," I said. "If I earned enough and you stopped working to raise the kids, would you hire a nanny to help?"

"Absolutely. A young stud, eager to please."

Olé. The woman (not the feminist) had left *mucha mierda* on Gutter Street that afternoon.

CITRIC LOVE

I was trying to convince my half orange how lucky she was to be married to me.

"Look, darling," I said. "I'm so wrapped up in my work that I don't have the energy or time, and forget about the money, to mess around on the side. When you see me pensive or distant, take it for granted that it's inspiration brewing. We writers are always on call. This keeps the temptations at bay."

She opened her mouth to comment, then thought twice. I felt proud to have made my point so succinctly.

Turned out she was just waiting for the opportune moment, which came the following day when I told her I was taking my laptop to the local bar.

"Right," she said. "Inspiration, not temptation. I should feel fortunate that you're off to a bar on Saturday afternoon, leaving me alone with the boys."

As life partners, we writers can be insufferable, always immersed in our own particular worlds, cudgeling our brains to find just the right word or image, sentence after sentence, until it adds up to a decent scene, only to find that what we have worked so hard to polish must ultimately be sacrificed for the whole. This constant squandering and winnowing takes its toll. And so we often jump the gun in the real world, putting our foot in it.

In telling this story, I have called my wife a nymph, a Nubian queen, and one of Charlie's Angels. I have likened her to a chunk of fruit, a weather vane, an Iberian bull, and a balloon. I have used her, against her will, to represent and symbolize Seville, Andalusia, and Spain. I have portrayed her—or so she claims—as lewd, coarse, and bossy. I have even gone so far as to make the quirks of our marriage public. But never once in our editing sessions did she try to censor me. Despite being used shamelessly for literary ends, she remains my number one fan.

What's worse, such unstinting support only means more work for her. In every spare moment, I have something else for her to read.

"*¡Qué hombre!*" (What a man!) she says. "*¡No me deja!*" (He doesn't leave me in peace!)

Never has a writer married so well.

One day, especially impressed by her editing suggestions, I said, "One of these days you're just going to have to sit down and write an article yourself."

She shook her head. "I lack the imagination."

"What does imagination have to do with it?" I said. "It's about talking straight. You're a natural at that. It's just a matter of getting used to a new medium. C'mon, I'll help you get started. Before we met, what did you think of *estadounidenses*?"

She shrugged.

"I didn't really have an opinion."

"First rule of the trade: don't duck the tough questions. C'mon. What did you think of us?"

While she collected her thoughts, I opened my notebook and uncapped my pen.

"Over-exaggerated, maybe," she said. "Prissy. A bit corny in your attention to detail."

"Good. Now we're talking. The excessively meticulous aspect is undeniable, yes. But what do you mean by over-exaggerated? How are we over-exaggerated? Expound a bit."

"I don't know…how you celebrate all the things you think you've achieved, as though civilization started with you. Or trotting out the flag every chance you get. Or those enormous university graduations with everyone throwing their caps in the air, like kids at a birthday party. Or how you all smile the same way, for no good reason, like you're advertising some orthodontics clinic."

"Fantastic examples. I told you you were a natural," I said, taking it all down. "And now, after being married and living with an

estadounidense for a handful of years, starting a family and all that, what do you think?"

She shrugged.

"*No se puede pedirle peras al olmo.*" (You can't ask an elm tree to produce pears.)

"What does that mean?"

"Basically that my first impressions were correct."

"*Me*, over-exaggerated?! Prissy and corny sometimes, I'll grant you that. But over-exaggerated in the ways you just mentioned? You know that any type of celebration makes me want to head for the hills. And smiling all the time? Aren't you always complaining about my long face? And patriotic, why? Because I don't like to see my national team disgraced in the World Cup?"

"You're over-exaggerated even when you sleep," she said.

"When I *sleep*? How in God's name am I supposed to sleep? Let me tell you something, it's you and *your* people who are over-exaggerated. All day in the street, smoking, drinking, going for *tapas*, oohing and aahing at the slightest novelty. The day they inaugurated the new trolley, Sevillians packed downtown as if *el Señor* himself were going to ride in it! And, okay, Sevillians aren't exactly patriotic, but you're parochial to the extreme. '*¡Sevilla es lo más grande!* (Seville is the greatest!) or '*¡En Sevilla se vive mejor!*' (In Seville we live better!) How many times have I had to hear that line of jingoistic crap rolling off some local's tongue? And let's not even talk about El Rocío, the April Fair, and Holy Week. Is there anything on earth more exaggerated than Your Sublime Mother Mary and Most Holy and Crowned Hope of Macarena? Sevillians actually think the neighborhood was named after her, not the other way around!"

"Relax, honey. I'm talking about your *way* of sleeping. With such abandon and intensity, like everything you do."

"And you? How do you sleep? Explain yourself. How does my Andalusian sleep?"

"These days, with my *noviocito.*"

Noviocito (itty bitty boyfriend) was her pet name for Wedge Two, who, at two years old, still did not have the slightest idea of what it meant to fall asleep by himself. Every night he occupied more of the marital bed, relegating his father with increasing frequency to the living room couch.

I closed my notebook and capped my pen. Chapter finished. She'd done it again!

My half orange: the half that makes me whole. Before her, I wobbled around in circles or fell facedown and got stuck to the floor. Now, finally attached to my formerly missing piece, I can roll, gain momentum, accomplish things. Without her, I'd rot or dry up, end up all pith and peel, drained of juice.

On that day when I was trying to convince her how lucky she was to be married to me, what I should have said was this:

"Honey, I'm so wrapped up in you and the wedges that I don't have the time, energy, and forget about the desire, to distract myself with foolishness. When you see me pensive or distant, take it for granted that I'm thinking of you and our children and what you all mean to me. Sometimes I dwell on things too much and don't show my appreciation. But, thanks to you, I've never been more present or attentive. Before you, I didn't know what I believed in. Now it's impossible to forget."

FATHERS

EL SEVILLANO

Around my in-laws' building, Wedge One became known as *El Sevillano*. He was a regular there because I would take him to visit almost every evening. His grandparents were in their eighties and not in the best of health, but they would forget their ailments while *El Sevillano* was around.

No matter how Wedge One ends up spending his life, even if—God forbid—he is led astray, he will still have done his share of good on earth just for having been present during this difficult final stage of his grandparents' existence. His grandma called him "*lo más grande*" (the greatest) and "*el niño de mi alma*" (the child of my soul). She taught him to clap his palms flamenco style, to open and close a Spanish fan with a flick of the wrist, and to plant kisses on a photo of Saint Angela of the Cross. My father-in-law did not do much more than doze at that point in his life, but at least when *El Sevillano* was visiting, he would open his eyes with a smile.

The neighborhood woman who coined Wedge One's nickname wasn't in the best of health either. As long as the weather was warm, her daughter would lead her across the courtyard to where a group of friends would sit in a circle of folding chairs watching the evening turn into night, talking about their aches and pains, their pills, the irregularity of their bowels, their children and grandchildren, their dogs, and finally, working themselves up into a lather of passions, about the hometown hopefuls competing on *Se llama copla*, an American Idol-style TV program spotlighting Spanish folkloric showtunes.

One day, without warning, Wedge One squatted down and planted a kiss on the rear end of this woman's dog. It was the first kiss I'd ever seen him give. The sensation must have pleased him because after that, if allowed, he would give a kiss to every dog that passed within lips' reach. As an alternative, he'd blow them kisses, another thing his grandma had taught him.

"*¡Sevillano! ¡Ven!*" (Sevillian! Come!) said the woman, and that's how he got the alias.

Wedge One's large Arab eyes, his thick, long lashes, and his dark skin are thanks to my half orange, but his fair, wavy hair, the light color of his eyes, and the Slavic cut to his features come from my side of the family. Since most people seem to focus on the physically different and overlook the physically commonplace, *El Sevillano* probably only appears Sevillian to my people. Basically, this woman dubbed him *El Sevillano* because he *didn't* look Sevillian. Finally, I was starting to catch on to the locals' sense of humor.

Upon being addressed this way, Wedge One would hold his ground for a moment. When it came to being smothered in love, he was, in his own mother's words, *arisco* (standoffish). But this woman always waited patiently. No pressure. Perhaps that's why he would eventually draw near, even if only to investigate her folding chair, which fascinated him. Her dog's water dish kept him interested, too. He liked to dunk his foot in it. Only while absorbed in such investigations would *El Sevillano* tolerate kisses and caresses.

Pretty soon we were stopping to chat every day. Or rather *El Sevillano* would stop, and I would chat. At that point, we were still in the phase of the father following the son's lead, instead of the other way around. Thanks to him, I would squat down to study ants swarming around sidewalk cracks, try to catch the leaves as they tumbled down from trees, stare at the moon, and count the stars.

The women would try to keep him in their circle as long as possible, using incentives like jingling keys or a cluster of dangling bracelets, or they would open a separate folding chair for him. If he wasn't allowed to climb up into it all by himself, he would abandon the circle immediately. In general, he preferred to be on the fringes with the dogs. *El Sevillano*'s favorite was a German shepherd named *Machote* (He-man), twice his size. My son would put his smiling, angelic face smack in front of He-man's black, panting snout, expecting a kiss.

When we would head upstairs to see his grandparents, *El Sevillano* would turn toward the women, raise his hand, and say "O!" (*¡Adiós!*), definitive proof that he was already speaking *andalú*.

Of course, *El Sevillano* had another set of grandparents in North Sutton, New Hampshire. We went to visit them from September to November, and *El Sevillano* became accustomed to a quieter routine. The wind rushing through the trees, a brook babbling beside the house, and the crunching of the gravel and early autumn leaves beneath his feet as he went for daily walks with my dad—that was about all the background noise he heard on that trip. When night fell, silence reigned and you could hear beavers gnawing at trees in the swamp out back and slapping at the water with their tails. After three months of this—15 percent of *El Sevillano*'s life at that point—we returned.

The buzz of our building intercom, the neighbors' raucous laughter as they gossiped on the landing, the blaring loudspeakers from vans selling pastries, potatoes, or the season's first oranges, still half green… all this had Wedge One on the verge of alarm for the first few days back home. And that was inside the house. As soon as we hit the streets in Madre de Dios, the cacophony of gunning motors and irate horns made him grab my hand and hold tight, something he'd never done before.

His Sevillian grandparents had worried they might not live to see him again, so I brought him by for a visit our first evening back. As we approached the building entrance, he stopped and looked to where the women used to sit during the spring and summer. Nobody was there. He reached out to me. I scooped him up and we stood for a moment, taking a united front against this foreignness.

A neighbor exited the building, holding the door open for us. I asked her about the women's whereabouts. She shrugged.

"These days, with the cold…"

The cold? We had just returned from morning frost and snow flurries.

We stepped inside the building. As the door began to shut, we heard something.

"*¡Mira! ¡El Sevillano! ¡Ven!*" (Look! The Sevillian! Come!)

We poked our heads back out. Sure enough, at the far end of the courtyard, along the arcade of hedges and orange trees, we glimpsed a waving hand.

"*¡El Sevillano ha vuelto! ¡Ven para acá, chiquillo! ¡Está aquí Machote! ¡Quiere darte un beso!*" (The Sevillian has returned! Come over here, kiddo! He-man's here! He wants to give you a kiss!)

Wedge One squirmed to be put down and then hit the ground running, on a beeline for his neighborhood fan club.

If people recognize you on the street, if they call out to you with joy, if they bestow a new name on you, their own creation, born of affection, wit, and native ways, this has to be a sign that you are at home and among your own, no?

Well, if my son is at home and among his own, then I am too.

ADIÓS TO THE REVEREND

I considered my father immortal. Perhaps every boy whose father has been happily implicated in his childhood feels that way. Or maybe, in my case, there was something extra behind the fantasy that he would never die.

In the years that he made his name in the newspaper business, through the '70s and early '80s, print media was still king. The average person kept up with current events by reading the papers and made sense of these events by reading the columnists. There was also television and radio, of course, but newspapers still broke the stories and then broke them down. From this prestigious and powerful podium, my dad stood out for expressing himself with humor, frankness, and clarity.

As a boy, not only did I see his image blown up as big as a movie screen on the sides of all *Daily News* trucks, I also saw the pile of fan letters that always sat backlogged on top of his desk, which he spent hours every weekend answering. But what really brought the sway of his influence home to me was seeing how the adult characters of my world—neighbors, teachers, the parents of my friends, and even the parish priest—would react to him, as if his presence transformed them into more interesting people. Something about the intensity of how he listened and the fullness of the attention he paid to people put them in top form.

For years I admired his success, basking in its advantages, and then in my teens I began to take it for granted, perhaps because he acted as though writing was just another way to make a living. If he didn't attach any special importance to it, then I wouldn't either. That all changed one morning while taking the bus to school, when I saw the man next to me burst out laughing while reading my dad's column. Without being physically present, he had been able to convulsively alter this complete stranger's emotional state. In that moment I understood the power of the well-written word. If my dad could use it to make people laugh, he could also use it to make them think and feel—and therefore act and change. From that point on, I wanted to do what he did.

At twenty-six years old, I got a job as a reporter at the *Staten Island Advance*, my hometown paper. By then, 1994, print journalism was not what it had been, although my dad was still a major player in it. He competed in another league than I did, but, even so, my job had a future; it was a solid first step, and my last name more or less ensured that I would not be overlooked.

It did not take long for me to realize that my pedigree had a downside. One day, a local soccer coach I was interviewing asked me if I was related to Bill Reel. I answered with unabashed pride that, yes, I was his son, and the coach replied, as if I were some cocky striker who needed to be taken down a peg, that I would never ever be the writer that my father was, that I should get that into my head right away. Bill Reel was one and only.

Of course he was. But I was, too. Everyone was.

I told myself that I would show this prick; I would show *all* the skeptics.

And so my ambition was born.

Family was everything to my father. All through his peak years as a columnist, he attended every one of his kids' ball games, even if we sat the bench. He drove us to practices, movies, or our friends' houses, then picked us up afterwards. As we grew older, he talked us through disappointments, took vacation days to drive us eight hundred miles to our college campuses each fall, and, in the summers, put aside his reading to listen attentively to our presumptions, problems, and plans, no matter how trite and overblown they must have seemed to him.

Because he listened with undivided attention—the exact skill that made him good at his job—my siblings and I believed in ourselves, maybe too much. In my twenties and early thirties, I was grateful for his emphasis on family because it gave me the confidence to choose the boldest path—to want more than he did, or so I thought.

Unlike him, I would put my career first, at least until I made my name. Both of us considered the novel a writer's highest calling. Every few years, he would start one, then abandon it midway through.

"Your old man lacks literary staying power," he concluded, apparently unfazed.

I thought if I could write a novel and be praised for it, that would silence the critics—especially the one in my head—once and for all. And so after three years in the newspaper business, I left it to focus on fiction.

But publication did not come easy; in fact, it did not come at all. Years passed and I didn't have a single published story to show. At a time when most other young adults had found their way and were living on their own, I was still at home, struggling at my outsized dream, cultivating a snide and pseudo-worldly wisdom, a kind of wise-cracking ennui that must have profoundly displeased my father. Yet this did not stop him from reading my long and lame attempts at literature, telling me the blunt truth about them while continuing to encourage me.

When I was thirty-two, finally living alone and enjoying single status to the max, I thought I had written a book that, although lighter fare, would gain me the fame and fortune I believed I so deserved: a hilarious (in my opinion) account of all my romantic exploits up to that point. As always, before pitching it to agents and editors, I asked him to help me, as I put it, "tighten up the prose."

I dropped off the manuscript. A week later, he stopped by my apartment, looking forlorn, to return it to me.

"The problem with the book isn't the prose," he said, easing himself into a chair. His back was acting up, a sure sign that he was stressed. "It's your thinking," he said.

"My thinking?" I said.

He stared bleary-eyed into the distance.

"Is it disorganized?" I asked.

He shook his head.

"Unclear?"

He fixed his eyes on mine.

"Puerile," he said. "From beginning to end."

He'd always been a stickler for the perfect word.

Before leaving my apartment, he said one last thing. "If you send this out, perhaps it'll get published. Who knows? But if it does, I think you'll end up regretting it forever."

Then he left, as though he had failed me. As much as I wanted to ignore his assessment, how could I, considering that it had come from love? I put the book aside, and when I looked at it again six months later, with my critical judgment unimpaired by either an inflated or a bruised ego, I had to stop reading out of shame for how my father must have felt. The book wasn't only puerile; it had been written by a pretentious jerk.

How many aspiring writers have been lucky enough to receive such sincere and expert criticism and thus be saved from themselves? Because he took me more seriously than my work, I learned that style and craft were pointless exercises if I did not live and think respectfully, trying to uphold a set of values exacting enough to keep me humble. All of my father's favorite advice about writing—"Avoid useless words," "Bless, don't impress," "It never gets easier, but you might get better at it"—also summed up his philosophy of life. It had never been about him, not if he could help it.

My father was way too modest about his own talents. "We columnists are craftsmen, not artists," he liked to say, then would disprove it the next day in the paper.

To take just one example, on September 7, 1977, when the controversy about removing any trace of Christianity from the New York public school curriculum was in the news, my dad published one of his masterpieces, "Can God Stand on His Head?", with my kid sister as the protagonist:

Just the other day…while I was driving to the hardware store to buy putty so my wife could patch a crack in our garage wall, Ursula, who was along for the ride, posed the kind of question she knew I could answer. I am never reluctant to talk about God, so it was a straight ball down the middle when Ursula asked, "Daddy, can God see what I'm thinking?"

I smiled to myself. What a precious child I have, I thought. Daddy's little girl. Only five years old, and already she's asking questions that would give pause to a bishop. My daughter the theologian.

"Yes," I told Ursula, "God can see what you're thinking. God is omnipotent. He can do anything. He can look right into your mind." Ursula thought this over briefly and came back. "How can God see through the roof of the car?"

This was not the follow-up question I had been expecting, but I didn't let it throw me. "I told you," I said. "God can do anything. He can even see through a roof. Nothing is impossible for God." I barely had time to admire the eloquence of my tag line when Ursula spoke up again. "Can God stand on His head?" she asked.

I considered pretending that I hadn't heard the question. I didn't want to subject God, not to mention myself, to the indignity of an answer. But having lived with Ursula for five years, I knew she would ask again, louder next time, so I said, "I'm sure God has better things to do, but the answer is yes, God can stand on His head if He wants to."

*You might think this would close the
subject, but no. Quick as a wink, Ursula asked,
"Without no hands?" Without no hands. Can
God stand on His head without no hands.
Ursula's grammar is worse than her theology.
Fortunately, at this point in the dialogue, we had
arrived at the hardware store. "Come along" I
told Ursula, "and help Daddy find the putty."
This challenge distracted her from matters
spiritual. God is merciful as well as omnipotent.*

*Anyway, Ursula is off to the first grade
tomorrow. She attends public school, where
discussion of God is forbidden. Lucky teachers.*

I keep a copy of the column beside my desk as a reminder
of the kind of writing I like best: profoundly simple and impossible
to dissect.

In 2005, just weeks before I left for Spain, doctors found a
malignant tumor in my father's neck. They were optimistic at first,
and he was, too. But even if the prognosis had been more dire, I
would not have changed plans, nor would he have expected me to.
I was about to take a definitive step, and, although neither he nor I
could possibly have known quite how definitive, we shared the
hunch that it was time for me to move out and away from my life. I
had been living on repeat for years, without personal or professional
prospects to revitalize me. Perhaps a stay abroad would give me a
boost. And so with my sails swelled by his approval and prayers, I
set off for faraway lands.

My desire to become a writer hadn't waned. I had kept at it,
day after day, year after year, and now knew a lot about reading and
writing, but it hadn't turned me into a writer yet—not a published
one, anyway—and I was nearly forty.

I came to Spain convinced that I would never settle down
and start a family. I'd decided that such a life was limiting and would
be too much for me to bear. To find substance outside of my work,

I would instead look to a new language and culture. Seville would be a clean slate upon which I could rewrite myself and then live with candor and abandon. And that's exactly what happened, but only after settling down and starting a family first.

A year and half after leaving for Seville, with my father's cancer in remission, I called to tell him that his first grandson had been conceived.

He burst out laughing.

"Susie," he said, passing the phone to my mother, "your son has good news."

When my parents finally met my half orange a few days before Christmas 2007, my father pulled me aside and said, "She's got the kind of wide-open smile that you can walk right into."

And be happy forever, I thought.

Two weeks later when he saw us off at the airport, he complimented her directly.

"You are now officially a member of my personal hall of fame," he said.

She had no idea what that meant, even after I tried explaining. She understood "Walk of Fame" though, which I figured was close enough.

Staring out the plane window, looking down at the cloud cover, she said, "It's clear that your father is totally in love with your mother."

Yes, I was in love with my half orange as much as my father was in love with his. Thanks to this woman with the wide-open smile, I had begun to find my way.

Even with the demands of family life, I still found time to go to cafés for a couple hours a day to scribble down impressions and anecdotes. For a while I noodled in Plaza Alfalfa, then in the Alameda de Hércules, and finally in Gran Plaza, closer to our apartment. One wedge soon became two, yet I managed to get work done.

Once, a man stopped next to my table and stared down at my notes.

"What are you studying?" he asked.

"I'm not studying," I replied. "I'm writing."

He shook his head and, raising his voice, tried again.

"What are you *studying?*"

"Estoy escribiendo," I repeated.

His eyes grew wide, then narrowed, and he left without saying another word.

Then it hit me. Writing had become studying, an attempt to understand this new world and language I was living in.

My father was back in chemotherapy by the time Wedge One made his first trip to the States in the summer of 2008. My father's best friend would later tell me that my dad had prayed every day to live long enough to meet my firstborn. Turned out he would live long enough to meet Wedge Two as well, born fourteen months later, and identical to my father in build and complexion.

By then, my father had another reason to be proud. One day I had sent off a half-dozen of my accumulated impressions and anecdotes to the *Diario de Sevilla.* The paper not only published them but asked me to write more. Soon I was given space every Saturday to chronicle my *guiri* adventures. There was my story and my face, staring back at me from my city's paper of record, just like my father's once had. The fact that I'd written the pieces in a language that he did not understand only added to his satisfaction.

"You had to move to another country and learn the language well enough to write in it in order to get the forum you deserve," he said.

That will always be the greatest compliment I've ever received.

On February 16, 2010, he wrote me his last email, with a final piece of advice: "What's of human interest, written with respect, humor, understanding, sympathy for the human condition—that's what makes the best columns, I believe."

Amen.

He died less than three months later, on May 3, in his own bed, as my brother held his hand and prayed the first prayer he had ever taught us: "God grant us the serenity to accept the things we cannot change, the strength to change the things we can, and the wisdom to know the difference." He was seventy-one. More than two hundred people attended his funeral in New London, New Hampshire, lots of them making the trip up from New York City. They did not speak about the fact that he had been, for many years, the most popular columnist of the most widely read newspaper in the United States, or that Frank Sinatra had been a fan, occasionally calling the city desk at the *News* to congratulate him, or that at least three New York mayors had tried, in vain, to curry his favor. As the mourners spoke to me about their experiences with him, three words kept popping up: humble, helpful, and wise. That day I discovered a lot about my dad that I had not known before, but what made me most proud was that they used to call him "Reverend" in the newsroom.

Living abroad, immersed in the happy family life that my father had always wanted for me, I missed the chance to be at his side during his final days. Because I was caught up raising my sons, spending the mornings with them while my half orange was at work, and teaching class and writing my columns in the afternoons—and also because I thought my father would never die—I hadn't been attentive to the details of his demise. To be honest, I hardly asked about them. My family called me home when he was already bedridden and barely conscious.

On the flight, to console myself for having lost not only the most important man in my life but also the opportunity to accompany him in his final stretch, I brought him back to life in words, words that would first appear in a newspaper as I exercised the profession that he'd left me as an inheritance.

When I got to my parents' place, too late, with the funeral already set, I discovered that I'd forgotten to pack dress shoes. Perhaps I thought I wouldn't need them.

"What size do you wear?" my mother asked.

We went down to the basement, where my father's shoes were lined up in a neat row at the bottom of the stairs. I tried on a

pair of his city shoes, the uppers nicely broken in but still shiny, and the soles and the heels worn down from walking. They fit perfectly. In the days that followed, I found myself striding out like him, with a bounce in my step and my feet pointed slightly outwards, open to the world.

I brought them back to Seville to see where they might lead me.

TO SPEAK IN GOLD

Heartbreak knows no borders, but perhaps we deal with it differently depending on where we're from and how we've been raised.

When my brother, sister, and I finished our college degrees, found jobs, and started to live on our own, our parents picked up and moved six hundred miles away to New Hampshire, as if their work were finally done. What's more, they left a few months after my sister had gotten married and had plans to start a family right away.

Joe, Ursula, and I saw nothing abnormal about this. We had always felt more than sufficiently loved. We'd been coddled, even smothered at times. The fact that we would be separated from our parents geographically for all but a few weeks of the year would not change the deep love and affection we felt for each other.

"When are you going to call your family?" my half orange often asks me.

When I first got to Spain, I called once a month, but it quickly became less. When I would call long distance, my voice could not express all that I wanted it to, and I would get off the phone feeling like I missed my family more, not less. My mother would fill the pauses with, "I don't want to keep you, sweetie…", or, "I know you're busy, dear…" Sometimes she would insist so much that I wondered if I was keeping *her*. Perhaps she felt the same as I did about talking on the phone. More likely she just wanted to relieve me of a burden.

It's different when we visit, staying in my brother's country house for a month every year. Joe takes off from work and travels up from New York to see us. Urs, her husband, and their growing brood drive up from New Canaan, Connecticut, and stay at my parents' place next door. With everyone physically present, that ten-acre patch of New Hampshire forest—"The Reel Family Compound," we call it—hums with the full family vibe.

But when separated by the Atlantic, I hardly keep in touch, because it's easier and because nobody pressures me to be a more attentive son, brother, or uncle. For a few years, my siblings and I gave each other's children Christmas presents, but then it got to be too much. Too many kids, too many gifts, too inconvenient. I suggested that we stop being so generous, to stave off holiday stress, and Joe and Ursula readily agreed.

In all Reel family encounters and communications, the underlying idea is to not abuse blood ties, to avoid having our love weigh on each other or make our individual lives more difficult than necessary. It's a philosophy of life and loving that I champion because it has great advantages. It provides freedom. If my parents' love were needy, I doubt I would have had it in me to try my luck in Spain, much less to settle here. When your parents follow their bliss and do their own thing, bending over backwards not to impose themselves on your choices, you're not only encouraged but inspired to live your own life. That's been my experience, anyway.

But there are disadvantages, too. When my uncle—my mother's only sibling—died, she did not mention it to Joe, Ursula, or me, probably because she hadn't wanted us to feel obligated to pull ourselves away from our busy, distant lives to go to the funeral. I can't fault her intentions. Even if she had told me, I wouldn't have returned for the funeral, and that would have added to my feelings of loss. But what else is a family for if not to be together while mourning, although some of us might only be present in spirit? Even sadder, as my father succumbed to cancer, both he and my mother kept me protected from the details, and so when he died, it felt sudden. He had been lucid in his final precarious weeks, had known they were his last weeks, and I would have liked to have been by his side, talking to him, gleaning bits of wisdom.

I want to be clear here. In my family's love dynamic, the onus is on the individual; we all understand that. Therefore, *my* choices, not my parents', deprived me of being at my father's side and having what might have been some of the most unforgettable and fruitful conversations of my life. In fact, more than anyone else in my family, I am the standard-bearer of this hands-off, better-not-to-know-until-I-absolutely-have-to kind of loving. I never once demanded updates about my father's health, never once insisted on knowing the truth, no matter how hard to hear. He said he was hanging in there, and that had been enough for me.

In stark contrast, there's my half orange's family. From the first moment, the difference *daba el cante* (sang out). While my family was overjoyed that I was "expanding my horizons" by dating someone from a faraway land, my future in-laws, especially the women, sized me up with great suspicion. They could not see beyond the fact that the youngest and most rebellious child of their clan was in love with a near forty-year-old foreigner, supposedly single, living thirty-five hundred miles from his homeland, with a suitcase of clothes and a laptop as his only belongings. They were convinced I was harboring dark, shameful secrets.

When I finally did manage to gain their trust, I realized I preferred their suspicion. At least then they had given me space. All of a sudden, they were dropping by without notice. Okay, my wife had just given birth and they wanted to lend a hand, and it was nice to know we could count on them. The thing was, we wanted to be alone—or I wanted us to be. My routine was sacred, and time was now scarcer than ever. The small talk made me want to scream. When we would visit her folks on Sundays, my mother-in-law, María, was always telling me what to do, what I had to eat, drink, and when it was time to cut my hair, when I had to shave, shine my shoes, and hand Wedge One back to her daughter. Once, María cast a scornful glance at my faded Levis and forced fifty euros on me so I would go out and buy myself a respectable pair of pants.

And God forbid her daughter not call her every day. Every day! And they had nothing to say. Half the time my wife hung up furious because all her mother had done was complain about how we never visited.

"It's like you live in Germany!" María would say, though we lived three miles away.

Germany was where the men had gone to work when the mines shut down in Villanueva del Río y Minas. To María, Germany was where loved ones lived if they lived far away. So that's where we lived, and where I was from: Germany, not New York.

To an *estadounidense* of my stripe, who had become accustomed to privacy and solitude after almost twenty years of single life, who had never had to answer to anyone or explain his habits and quirks, such an onslaught of unrelenting advice, concern, and demands seemed more like hostility than love.

Then my father-in-law got sick. In a matter of months, Luis could no longer walk or get up out of his armchair. This sudden falloff occurred when my half orange was pregnant with Wedge Two. Because she had bled a few times in the early months of carrying and doctors had told her to go easy or we could lose the baby, my sister-in-law, Luisa, took on the brunt of caring for Luis, arriving every morning to get him out of bed, then bathe, shave, and dress him. She kept the fridge stocked, organized doctor visits, and helped to administer his battery of pills, putting them in Dixie cups and marking them, so María, over eighty and not in the best of shape either, would not get confused.

Feeling bad that the caretaking duties seemed excessively one-sided, I half-heartedly volunteered to put Luis to bed at night so that at least Luisa would have her evenings free. Putting Luis to bed would be the least of it, I thought. The real work and drudgery would be sitting down with my in-laws every night, trying to carry on some kind of coherent and flowing conversation. My Spanish continued to be lacking, at least while conversing with them. To top it off, María was hard of hearing, although with everybody else I had ever seen her with, she managed quite well through intuition and lip-reading.

"I'm willing to do this," I told my wife, "but if your mom starts laying a guilt trip on me, saying why don't we ever bring the kids over, do we think this is the proper way to treat family, blah

blah blah, I'm gonna go into robot mode, steering your dad around her like she's a piece of furniture."

That nightly visit to my in-laws changed almost immediately into the only time of day in which I did not doubt for a moment that I was doing something essential—essential, most of all, for me. I know people who have cared for bitter, insulting, and even violent loved ones and have done it with understanding and affection. If day after day, the work you do with heart, soul, and grit not only goes unappreciated but is derided and demeaned by the very person you lovingly care for, yet you carry on undeterred and unresentful, that's truly worth admiration. But caring for Luis was nothing like that. He suffered from a kind of Parkinson's disease that either provoked or went hand-in-hand with increasing bouts of senile dementia. His system was shutting down gradually, but not so gradually that he and I and everybody else were not alarmed by how relentlessly the sickness was advancing. Holding a glass, talking, or even swallowing became harder for him every day. His decline could not be curtailed, yet he never once complained.

"If your dad only complained a bit," I said to my half orange, "then we'd know how to take better care of him."

On my way in and out of my in-laws' building, I would run into neighbors who knew that Luis was wasting away.

"If only you'd known him before!" they would say.

If only you knew him now! I would think.

Sometimes Luis and I would chat about Sevilla FC. He had always been a big fan, spending the day listening to sports talk radio on his beat-to-hell, battery-powered transistor. Sometimes he would mention a match that had occurred years ago as though it had happened that afternoon. Diego Maradona's name would pop up; he had played for Sevilla in the twilight of his career, years after his controversial goal in the '86 World Cup—scored, as he put it, "*con la mano de Dios*" (with the hand of God)—had made him the most famous soccer player in the world. Other times Luis would get all worked up about a dish of rabbit or lamb that he had cooked up in his dreams and would invite me to partake in the feast. I would graciously accept. He had been a cook in the military and in hospitals, retiring after a kitchen accident burned him from the back of his head down to his tailbone. According to my wife, his mantra at the family table had been "*¡Come y calla!*" (Eat and shut up!), and, when he did not say it, he preached by example. If María invited a neighbor in to chat before Sunday lunch or over coffee and cake, Luis would mumble, "*Siempre tenemos un testigo de vista a la hora de comer.*" (We've always got an eye-witness on hand when it's time to eat.) He had grown up in *Las Minas* with enough learning and *picardía* (street savvy) to hold his own and make a living when a lot of young Spanish men were forced to take on backbreaking and humiliating work to support their families. My half orange recalled with a wry smile how he would return from the night shift at the cement factory—where he worked before moving the family to Seville—with a bouquet of flowers picked from rich people's gardens on the walk home, so she could bring them to school as a gift for the nuns. Luis was proud to have never tried pizza or Coca Cola, to have never worn a pair of jeans. "*¿Pa' qué?*" (What for?) he would say. The youngest of six brothers, he hardly remembered his father, who had died young. Some days when I would arrive for my visit, Luis would think he was back in the personnel office at the cement factory and offer to give me a tour.

But for the most part, we didn't speak. Our time together was marked and measured by the steps we took to get him ready for and into bed. I was a beginner in this kind of silence, a manly silence, charged with feelings all the more potent for going unspoken. Before meeting him, I had only known how to be completely and comfortably silent alone.

There is a Spanish idiom, *hablar en plata* (to speak in silver), which means to get right to the point. If you combine that with the English phrase "silence is golden," then most of the time Luis and I spoke in gold.

Although not being at my father's side during his final weeks meant I might have missed out on some of the most important conversations of my life, by helping to care for my father-in-law during his two-year illness, I gained some of the most important silences of my life. I discovered that words were superfluous when it came to dying a drama-free and supremely dignified death.

When I arrived for our nightly ritual, María would greet me with something along the lines of, "*No hay quien te pague esto, hijo mío.*" (There is no way to repay you for this, son of mine.) Then she would lead me by the hand to Luis, who would be dozing in his armchair.

"*Fuentes!*" she would shout, using his last name, grabbing the lapels of his house robe and beating the breadcrumbs off him. "*Está aquí John. No le entretengas. Le están esperando la Virginia y los niños.*" (John's here. Don't hold him up. Virginia and the boys are home waiting.)

When my work was finished twenty or thirty minutes later, María would lead me to the kitchen and try to give me all the groceries that Luisa had filled the fridge and fruit bowl with that morning. My mother-in-law, who so loved and thrived on daily contact with neighbors and shopkeepers, hardly left the house, except to take out the garbage and go to her doctor, for the whole of her husband's illness. She was, despite her own growing list of ever more debilitating ailments, a constant source of motivation and encouragement for her slowly perishing lifelong love. The only thing she lamented was that I hadn't known Luis in his physical prime.

"*¡Lo apañado y fuerte que era! ¡Un hombre de postín! ¡Como tú! ¡La vida cómo es!*" (How handsome and strong he was! A man you could show off! Like you! What a life this is!)

One night, when Luis was more alert and talkative than usual, he asked me if I had met his younger daughter. Before I could remind him who I was, he began to sing my half orange's praises, clearly insinuating that we should get to know each other. He went so far as to say, "*Tiene muy buen cuerpo la chiquilla.*" (She has a really good body, the girl does.)

Reward reaped. Summit reached. Distinction earned. The yearning and avid disciple had finally received the highest of all possible accolades from his wise and laconic master. I felt as though

King Lear, in a moment of lucidity, had just offered me the hand of Cordelia.

Then everything changed again. After two years of waiting and of caring for Luis as a family, Andalusian Social Services finally responded, and he was assigned three daily visits by trained caretakers. From one day to the next, our nightly ritual ceased. Now when I would visit with his daughter and grandchildren on Sundays, Luis would be dozing like before, but nobody made an effort to wake him. I actually came to prefer that he was unaware of my presence, or of who I was, because, without our routine, without the steps we had once taken to get him ready for the night, I did not know how to act around him. Our silences now felt leaden, not golden. I found myself looking for excuses not to visit—I had classes to prepare, report cards to write, columns to submit—so that I would not feel lost and useless around him.

One Sunday, I could not get out of the weekly visit. When we arrived, I saw immediately how much he had deteriorated since my last visit. He could no longer speak. He was afraid to swallow, afraid the food would get caught in his throat. The Spanish verb *violentar*, "to apply violent means to overcome resistance," is often used to describe internal strife. That day more than any other day, my presence around Luis *me violentaba* (tore me up inside). Finally, out of desperation, I put my hand in his, like we had done so often during our nightly ritual. He responded with chilling force, with a kind of death grip that seemed to close around my lungs as much as my hand. I withstood it as long as I could, then pretended that Wedge One was calling me from the living room, so I could wrench my hand out of Luis's and flee to take in great gulps of air.

He would die in his sleep a few weeks later.

No wonder we go out of our way not to disturb the colossus of feelings lurking in our depths. Once it's stirred into action, we're never the same again. Perhaps we're enhanced, but we feel diminished.

Taking care of Luis for as long as I did and then being deprived of the privilege helped verify for me a truth that in my half orange's family is a way of life: love is born and thrives *thanks to*—not despite—the burdens and obligations that it imposes upon us.

Family ties are abused as much when you yank on them as when you don't. That's the lesson I learned: that love is no less crushing either way.

"Sometimes I think you came into my life to care for my father," my half orange once said, when I was still a beginner in this new way of loving and would go every night to be enlarged by Luis's generosity of spirit.

What's certain is that, had I not come into her life, I would never have known what it meant to care for a father.

ALL SOULS AT CHRISTMAS

Returning to Seville after my father's funeral in the spring of 2010, I felt as if his spirit, freed of the cage of his body, could finally accompany me thirty-five hundred miles away. For a while, I actually missed him less than when he was alive.

But then when I returned to the States with my half orange and the wedges seven months later to celebrate Christmas, his spiritual presence, which had felt so close in recent months, vanished around so many remnants of his physical presence: his reading chair empty, the basket beside it stuffed with magazines that would soon stop coming in the mail; his stash of Earl Gray decaffeinated tea still filling the cabinet above the stove; the Charlie Parker and Dave Brubeck CDs stacked atop the stereo. For the first time, I felt abandoned, and the only person I could talk to about it was my wife. Although she was an official member of his personal hall of fame, she had hardly known him. She had burst into tears upon learning that he died though, more moved by the loss than I seemed to be.

After that first Christmas dinner without him, she asked me why there had been no prayer or moment of silence dedicated to him before eating.

"We said grace," I said. "We all thought of him then."

"I'm sure you did, but why not mention him?"

I shrugged. "It would have been awkward."

"Awkward?"

"As a family, we just don't gush about sad stuff, not around each other," I said.

I could see that she didn't understand. At the funeral, only my mom had wept openly, in sporadic moments, then would immediately get a hold of herself again. Later, in search of solace, she found a bereavement group but had only gone to one meeting.

"The woman in charge put sappy music on and read maudlin poems. The point seemed to be to get us all to cry," she'd said.

"Each of us prefers to mourn in private," I explained to my wife. "But don't think that, just because we keep our composure around each other, we're trying to avoid how we really feel."

"I know," she said. "It's just that, because your mother controls herself so much, I feel like I've got to give her space, and I'd like to tell her how sorry I am about your dad's death and to offer whatever consolation I can."

"Yeah," I said. "I know how you feel."

Despite being seventy years old, my mother would pass at least an hour a day on the paths of the natural reserve behind the house. My parents had gone for regular walks there when my dad was still well enough. Now, in midwinter, not even a blizzard could detain her. She would strap on snowshoes or cross-country skis and go out into that white wilderness alone, to be with him, I was sure— proof that she was not bottling anything up, but perhaps also proof that she would have liked to talk about things in her own way. Alone in her house, recently widowed, she had spent months choosing just the right natural gravestone for the man she had been happily married to for forty-six years. She had finally found the perfect one out back—not too big, not too small, with a flat space for an engraving—then had asked a neighbor to come in with his backhoe and pickup truck to unearth it and transport it to remote West Part Cemetery, where my dad had chosen to have his ashes buried. The stone hadn't been in place for the funeral in May, but now it was, with a commemorative plaque. I was curious to see it. If only everything had not been under three feet of snow.

Then I recalled the recent autumn holidays in Seville, celebrated just two months before: All Saints' Day and All Souls' Day. On those back-to-back *fiestas solemnes*, Sevillians gathered in the cemetery with buckets of soap and water to clean loved ones' graves. I decided to do the same at Christmas, except with a shovel and broom.

A few days later, my half orange and I drove our rental car through a windswept snowscape of dormant farmland and leafless forest, then parked beside a six-foot-high snowbank in front of an opening in the cemetery's stone wall. I got the shovel and broom out of the trunk, shut it, then climbed the snowbank, pulling my wife up after me. From there, we could see the crooked rows of graves running down the side of a gently sloping hill. Most of the tombstones were just bumps in the blanket of snow. Only the taller and more ostentatious ones poked up out of it, each sporting a jagged-edged cap of snow. No shoveled paths or footprints could be distinguished. Clearly, we were the first people here since the big snows had hit. My father's grave was near the bottom of the incline, and we headed toward it, our legs sinking thigh-deep into the snow. I held the broom and shovel up over my head, as though wading through a flood. The temperature had maxed out for the day at ten degrees Fahrenheit. As we descended into a dell, the wind died down and only our crunching footsteps and vigorous breathing could be heard.

I found the crab apple tree that my mother had planted near the grave and began digging in a three-yard radius around it. The work kept me warm. But after about forty-five minutes, with the circle completed and the three-yard radius extended by another three yards, I was sweating hard and still hadn't hit on the stone. Meanwhile, my poor half orange. To her, sixty-five degrees was cold, and here she was, teeth chattering, shrunken into her shell of goose down, polar fleece, and wool, refusing to complain out of respect for my way of mourning. The huge white hole I had dug into the drift at the base of the hill could have been another grave. We stood at the bottom of it with that tiny bare tree in the center, staring up at the tips of the high forest branches scraping the bone gray sky.

"Let's come back tomorrow," I said.

The next day, I returned with only my mother. Thanks to her daily hikes behind the house, she had no problem leading the

way from the road to the grave. She even broke away from the footprints that we had left the day before, blazing her own trail. At the edge of the hole around the crab apple tree, she stopped to admire the neat, high rim of snow. The structure looked more stable today, less likely to collapse back in on itself.

"Wow," she said. "A yeoman's job. You missed the stone by inches." She took the shovel and broom from me, stepped forward and began chipping away at the wall of snow. I let her do the work, with her usual brio. When I was a kid, she had rarely let me help with housework.

"Thanks, sweetie, I can do it faster on my own," she'd say.

When the stone was mostly cleared, she squatted to brush off the last bits of snow with her gloved hands.

"There," she said. "What do you think?"

I squatted next to her, placing my hand on top of the stone. Only the tip seemed to rise out of the earth, with the bulk of it buried. I thought of Hemingway's "iceberg theory" about writing, which my dad had always adhered to: "Let the reader imagine what's below," he would say. The plaque was black, with the inscription in gold: William J. Reel, 1939-2010. A small engraved illustration showed a quill lying beside an overturned ink bottle to commemorate his career as a columnist.

"The crab apple tree blooms in May," my mother said.

My father had died in May.

"It was cultivated in Connecticut," she said.

My parents had been born and raised there and had met in New Haven, when my father was at Yale and my mother at Albertus Magnus.

"I planted another one right in front of the house," she said. "The deer and moose love its fruit."

I continued to stare at the illustration.

"The burial plot is big enough so that we can all fit in it," she said. "And your spouses, too."

"What drawing would you like on your stone, Mom?" I finally asked.

She took a moment to consider the question.

"Perhaps a vacuum cleaner," she said, "which you can bury with me."

We burst out laughing—just the two of us wracked by emotion, the happy kind, bouncing off that barren landscape, bringing back my dad's spirit, stronger than ever.

A year later, on December 29, 2011, Luis would pass away, also in his bed, dreaming away, watched over by loved ones. I had the honor to write his epitaph:

"*Dedicó la vida a su familia y murió junto a ella.*" (Dedicated his life to his family and died at their side.)

The words are carved into black marble, beside a simple silver cross. The Spanish sounds better and makes me think of them both, although they never met on earth.

EPILOGUE

IN GOD'S GARDEN

In Seville, a little voice follows me and repeats, *"¡Qué suerte tienes! ¡Qué bien vives! ¡Qué suerte!"* (How lucky you are! How well you live! What luck!)

Growing up, I was always suspicious of luck. My people and my nation downplay it when recognizing our feats. We believe in the self-made hero, that we control destiny and not the other way around. We might consider a weekend in Vegas fun, but winning big there doesn't garner admiration unless we've outsmarted the system. To call something a fluke is to disparage it.

Sevillians see luck differently. When someone is fired, they're likely to say, *"No ha tenido suerte."* (He had no luck.) I'm more likely to recall that old saw, "You have to make yourself indispensable," implying that the setback might have been avoided. If Real Betis Balompié loses after a well-played match, a typical fan comment is, *"No tuvimos suerte con el gol."* (Unlucky before the goal.) I shake my head and think, "Nah, we blew it." My Sevillian acquaintances have the habit of summing up a Don Juan by saying, *"Tiene mucha suerte con las mujeres."* It's true that a guy can get lucky sometimes, but if it happens again and again, then clearly he has the magic touch.

I remember how furious my New York buddy John, a successful model, got at his wedding when a drunk guest, frustrated about his own professional and personal stagnancy, said to him, "You won the genetic lottery, dude." The insinuation that John's career and romantic success were due merely to the good fortune of a sculpted physique and a handsome face offended him, and rightly so, I believe.

When Sevillians claim that I am lucky to like my work and be free of debts, to have considerate kids and an understanding wife,

I have to resist the urge to snap back, "Luck's got nothing to do with it."

In the States, wealth, professional status, and even a happy family life are regularly attributed to some combination of talent, mettle, and know-how—a potentially problematic way of thinking because if you take credit for the triumphs, then you also have to take the blame for falling on your face.

Surely that's why it rubs me wrong when Sevillians point out my luck. If for so many years I chalked up my lack of a serious love life and rewarding work to not knowing the best way to make use of my talents, I don't want anyone coming along to question my achievements now that I've made some progress.

I was born in a developed democratic country, into a family with the resources, knowledge, and zeal to raise and educate me well. I have always enjoyed good mental and physical health. I have never been preyed on by the deceitful or the depraved. My loved ones and I have never been victims of natural disasters or been in the wrong place at the wrong time when innocent bystanders were being swept away.

When I arrived in Seville to make a go of it, I did not come up against prejudices, at least not regarding my competence and capabilities. In fact, because of my nationality and the color of my skin, I was immediately, undeservingly, assumed to be a cut above the other immigrant groups, and perhaps even the Spaniards themselves. I only had to respect the language and customs, an attitude that came naturally to me, and I was almost unanimously accepted. I lived the entire immigrant cycle—estrangement, struggle to subsist, struggle to assimilate, and integration—in three years instead of three generations, and all the while with a safety net, because the privileged world I had been born and raised in was always waiting for me back home.

For all this, I must count myself fortunate. But my current life in Seville is also thanks to guts and perseverance, although surely others have sacrificed, endured, and overcome more than I have in their attempt to assimilate, without the same results.

While still courting my half orange, I once asked her, "How is it possible that you're pushing forty and have never found happiness in love?"

She shrugged and replied, "I was about to get angry at the world."

I was pushing forty and trying not to get angry at myself. Where I was born and raised, anyone who fails to find love not only has to live with the loneliness but also with the culturally imposed idea that he or she had somehow asked for it. The Sevillian idea that we all just have to live the lot we have been cast is more humane, if perhaps less ambitious.

My native culture drummed home that I could be whatever I wanted, as long as I wanted it badly enough. That's an inspiring way to see the future when you're young. But if you age and are still not what you've always dreamed of becoming, then, after taking stock of yourself, you should probably find a less demoralizing philosophy of life.

Here's my philosophy of life: *sevillana seviyorkino Sevilla.* It all runs together, like a prayer recited under my breath. My *sevillana* comes first, because she's more important to me than the place. Plus, our *sevillanitos* were born of her. But really it's all one and the same, a conglomeration of people and cultures living in constant and mostly happy tension, with me in the middle, carried along.

The Giraldillo, that 1.2-ton statue of a woman warrior representing faith that crowns the bell tower of the Seville Cathedral, calls to mind a different statue of a woman, equally emblematic, a monolith of maternal strength for the "tired," the "poor," and the "huddled masses." My half orange, my Lady Liberty, took me in, gave me a new language, a new family, and a new way to see the world, allowing me to be reborn.

The all-American part of me wants to say, "I changed my life to come to Seville." But that's not true. I came to Seville and it changed my life, thanks to you-know-who.

My favorite Spanish idiom is *De todo hay en la viña del Señor*. In English we'd say, "It takes all sorts," or, "To each his own," but the literal translation is far better:

In God's garden, everything grows.

I stumbled upon the right fruit here and my half fits hers perfectly.

Sure, I am partly responsible for my happiness, but I've also been lucky, extremely lucky. I hope Sevillians never let me forget it.

ACKNOWLEDGMENTS

My mother, a force of nature, instilled in me the staying power and resolution for this *camino del escritor*, and my father the humility, insight, and craft.

El maestro Glenn Stout helped bring the early drafts of this story to another level; Ellen Wilson Fielding's sharp eye and deft hand helped cut away excess; Gerald Brennan and Lauren Gioe at Tortoise Books provided indispensable advice and insight in the final stretch; and my *compadre* Lewis Dimmick was always there in a pinch.

Valga la redundancia if I again thank my half orange, Virginia Fuentes Valencia. *Vaya tela lo que la chiquilla tiene que aguantar día tras día. Tiene el cielo ganado.*

Finally, this book wouldn't be the same without the illustrations of Daniel Rosell. The only downside of not reproducing my story in the order that it first appeared in *Diario de Sevilla* is losing the transformation that my character made in Daniel's work. The upstart Yank was clearly growing on him. How this encouraged me!

Semana 11   Semana 26   Semana 45

ABOUT THE AUTHOR

John Julius Reel moved from Staten Island to Seville in 2005. His memoir, *¿Qué pinto yo aquí?* (Where do I fit in?), was published in 2014 by Editorial Confluencias in Spain. He is a regular participant in various *tertulias* on Andalusian public radio, has dabbled in acting, most notably in Nonio Parejo's feature film *6 toreros yankees 6*, and has published over one hundred articles in Spanish newspapers. He loves teaching. His Facebook page *Spanglish in a Minute* and his Instagram account @johnjuliusreel have over two hundred thousand combined followers. He also passionately reviews memoirs on his YouTube channel *Book Rants*. *My Half Orange* is his first book in English.

ABOUT TORTOISE BOOKS

Slow and steady wins in the end – even in publishing. Tortoise Books is dedicated to finding and promoting quality authors who haven't yet found a niche in the marketplace – writers producing memorable work that will stand the test of time.